Planet Phonics
Kniteracy

by Debbie Long

Outhouse
PUBLISHING

First published in the UK
by Outhouse Publishing
Copyright © Deborah Long
and Outhouse Publishing Ltd 2012

Author
Debbie Long

Co-creator and educational advisor
Jill Hassan

Knitting consultant
Laura Long

Illustrations
Pip Adams

Designer and photographer
Becky Hill

Publisher and editor
Fiona McWilliam

British Library Cataloguing in Publication Data. A catalogue
record for this book is available from the British Library

ISBN 978-0-9572391-1-1

Printed and bound in England by Butler Tanner and Dennis

With special thanks to Carol Wilson for checking all the
patterns, and to our lovely models Alannah, Ben and Oscar.

Contents

Planet Phonics – an introduction 6

Phonics explained 10

Knitting Patterns............................... 12

Planet a – the sneezing planet 12

Baby bear 14

Clicking cat 16

Dancing dinosaur................................ 18

Planet e - the exciting planet 20

Freezing frog.................................... 22

Growling gorilla 24

Huffing horse 26

Planet i – the itching planet.......................... 28

Jumping Jack.................................... 30

Kicking kitten 32

Licking lion 34

Munching monkey 36

Nodding nurse.................................. 38

Planet o – the orange octopus planet.................. 40

Popping pig 42

Quiet queen 44

Running robot 46

Silly snake 48

Ticking tiger 50

Planet u – the upside down planet 52

Val the vet 54

Wild witch 56

Alien x 58

Yawning Yasmin 60

Zooming zebra....................................... 62

The Planet Phonics telephone 64

The Planet Phonics rocket 66

Useful Information............................70

Knitting know-how............................71

Templates 74

Letter templates 94

Planet Phonic Games.........................96

Planet Phonics...
an introduction

Once upon a time there was a mouse...

and this was the start of Planet Phonics

Every week Jill Hassan, a Brighton-based infant school teacher, and her friend Debbie Long, a special needs teacher and knit designer, would get together for a knitting lesson.

With the help of her daughter Laura's book 'Toy Tales', Debbie was teaching Jill how to knit. With lots of practise Jill eventually created a little mouse.

While knitting and chatting Jill mentioned that she was teaching the sound 'sh' to her class of reception children. Together Jill and Debbie jokingly came up with the name for the mouse: 'shy Sheila'.

The following day Jill proudly took shy Sheila into school and showed her to the class. The children loved and played with her and quickly learnt the sound 'sh'.

A bed was made for the mouse and if the class became too noisy the children said 'Shush, you'll wake shy Sheila'. Debbie and Jill realised they were on to something big and over the next few months they developed the knitted characters that make up Planet Phonics.

In 'Planet Phonics Kniteracy' the 26 letters of the alphabet have been turned into easy-to-knit characters. Our knitted characters are soft, tactile and hard wearing, and will appeal to children as well as adults.

They include five brightly coloured balls (the planets) which represent the vowels a, e, i, o, and u. The 21 consonants are each represented by an unforgettably appealing person or animal.

It was really important to make the vowels different from the rest of the knitted characters. Vowels are in almost every word and it is necessary that children realise their role and vital importance in words.

Each character has its own story, a rhyme and action. Planet a (with the a pronounced like the a in apple), for example, is the sneezing planet; land here and beware of sneezing yourself away:

Bud the baby bear is the character for b. He is so small that he finds it hard to get up and down stairs so he 'b, b, b, bumps' himself down them.

The character for t is Tom the ticking tiger. He has swallowed a clock so instead of roaring goes 't, t, tick tock'; yawning Yasmin has been up all night playing with her yo-yo and she can't stop 'y, y, y, yawning'.

At the back of the book (page 94) are photocopiable letters designed to fit into the knitted pockets on the back of each character. There are also some simple games to play with children using the knitted characters. Patterns for a 'phone and a rocket have been included, along with rhymes and games to go with them. The characters fit inside the rocket and the rhymes and games mean that they can be introduced in an exciting way. You can call up to Planet Phonics on the 'phone and an individual character is sent down in the rocket.

Planet a can make you sneeze,
And all the apples blow off the trees.
a, a, a, atishoo

The accompanying action is pretending to sneeze while saying 'a, a, a, atishoo'.

Planet Phonics knitting patterns will appeal to knitters of all abilities and all ages. The characters are simple and quick to knit, and this book includes an illustrated guide for novice knitters, starting on page 71.

Teachers can make the characters or get help to make them to use as a teaching aid. Parents can make them as play objects but also to help their children to learn the phonics which will lead to them reading. Grannies can knit them for their grandchildren or for their local school. Children who are learning to knit can have a go at making them. In fact anyone can knit them just for fun.

The patterns have been designed to be knitted without any restrictions on yarns or sizes. If you are a loose knitter the toys will be bigger than those made by tight knitters but this doesn't matter. The patterns tell you to use a double knitting yarn but the make of yarn used doesn't matter. Just remember, the softer the yarn the cuddlier the character.

The patterns show the characters in particular colours but it doesn't really matter what colours you use. Each toy is made out of just one or, at most, two balls of wool and are a great use for left-over yarn.

Knitting is becoming more and more popular. A craft that a few years ago was considered very unfashionable is again trendy, and knitting clubs are springing up everywhere. Groups meet in pubs, cafés and people's houses.

With 'Planet Phonics Kniteracy' we hope to encourage the formation of knitting clubs in schools, for making the characters that children can then use in class. Groups could be set up in old people's homes, helping bridge the gap between young and old.

In September 2011, statistics from the Department for Education suggested that nearly a fifth of all seven-year-olds are failing to reach level 2 – the standard expected of this age group – in reading and writing. The problem continues into junior schools, where according to the Department of Education, a fifth of 10- and 11-year-olds are failing to reach the required literacy levels for their age. A learning support teacher, working in primary schools in Brighton, thinks that the problem is actually much worse than the statistics suggest and Christine Gilbert, head of Ofsted, has said that standards of reading and writing among many 11-year- olds fall "stubbornly short of achievable levels".

All children should be taught how to decode words in order to read.

Planet Phonics knitted characters have been developed to make learning to read a multi-sensory process and, most importantly, to make it fun and appealing to children of all ages, including those with special educational needs. Planet Phonics empowers parents to help their children to learn the phonics necessary for them to become readers, through stories, rhymes, actions and play.

Phonics explained

Phonics is a method of teaching reading and writing using letter sounds. It works on the ability of the child to hear, identify and then blend sounds into words.

The English language is extremely complicated. We know there are 26 letters in the alphabet and most of us have recited or sung the alphabet to learn the order of the letters. Reciting the alphabet teaches us the letter names. In phonics we concentrate on the sounds that the letters make.

In 'Planet Phonics Kniteracy', the sounds of the 26 letters are given a character, a name, an action and a rhyme. The vowels are particularly important and these are the five planets.

a The a in Planet a is pronounced as the 'a' at the beginning of apple.

b The b is pronounced like the 'b' in bear.

c The c is pronounced like the 'c' in cat.

d The d is pronounced like the 'd' in dinosaur.

e The e in Planet e is pronounced as the 'e' at the beginning of egg.

f The f is pronounced like the 'f' in frog.

g The g is pronounced like the 'g' in gorilla.

h The h is pronounced like the 'h' in horse.

i The i in Planet i is pronounced as the 'i' at the beginning of insect.

j The j is pronounced like the 'j' in j jump.

k The k is pronounced like the 'k' in kitten.

l The l is pronounced like the 'l' in lion.

m The 'm' is pronounced like the 'm' in monkey.

n The 'n' is pronounced like the 'n' in nurse.

o The 'o' in 'Planet o' in pronounced as the 'o' at the beginning of orange.

p The 'p' is pronounced like the 'p' in pig.

q The 'q(u)' is pronounced like the 'q(u)' in queen.

r The 'r' is pronounced like the 'r' in robot.

s The s is pronounced like the 's' in snake.

t The t is pronounced like the 't' in tiger.

u The u in Planet u in pronounced as the 'u' at the beginning of up.

v The v is pronounced like the 'v' in vet.

w The w is pronounced like the 'w' in witch.

x The x is pronounced like the 'x' in x-ray.

y The y is pronounced like the 'y' in yawn.

z The z is pronounced like the 'z' in zebra.

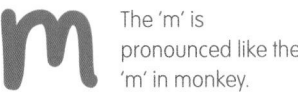

These sounds can be blended together to make simple words.

For example the sounds c-a-t can be blended together to make the word cat.

The sounds p-i-g can be blended together to make the word pig.

Or the sounds h-e-n can be blended together to make the word hen.

Planet a
The sneezing planet

Out in space, but not too far away is a planet – Planet a.
It's not known as the sneezing planet for nothing. Anyone or anything that lands on its surface starts to sneeze within minutes – a, a, a, atishoo.

Knitting pattern to make Planet a

Cast on 9 sts
Row 1: [kfb, k1] repeat x 4, k1 (13sts)
Row 2: p
Row 3: [kfb, k1, kfb] repeat x4, k1 (21sts)
Row 4: p
Row 5: [kfb, k3, kfb] repeat x4, k1 (29sts)
Row 6: p
Row 7: [kfb, k5, kfb] repeat x4, k1 (37sts)
Row 8: p
Row 9: [kfb, k7, kfb] repeat x4, k1 (45sts)
Row 10: p
Row 11: [kfb, k9, kfb] repeat x4, k1 (53sts)
Row 12: p
Row 13: [kfb, k11, kfb] repeat x4, k1 (61 sts)
Row 14: p
Row 15: [kfb, k13, kfb] repeat x4, k1 (69sts)
Row 16: p
Row 17: [kfb, k15, kfb] repeat x4, k1 (77 sts)
Row 18: p
Stocking stitch for 12 rows
Row 31: k1 [k2tog, k14, skpo, k1] repeat x4 (69sts)
Row 32: p
Row 33: k1 [k2tog, k12, skpo, k1] repeat x4 (61sts)
Row 34: p
Row 35: k1 [k2tog, k10, skpo, k1] repeat x4 (53sts)
Row 36: p
Row 37: k1 [k2tog, k8, skpo, k1] repeat x4 (45sts)
Row 38: p
Row 39: k1 [k2tog, k6, skpo, k1] repeat x4 (37sts)
Row 40: p
Row 41: k1 [k2tog, k4, skpo, k1] repeat x4 (29sts)
Row 42: p
Row 43: k1 [k2tog, k2, skpo, k1] repeat x4 (21sts)
Row 44: p
Row 45: k1 [k2tog, skpo, k1] repeat x4 (13sts)
Row 46: p
Thread yarn through stitches and pull tight.

Pocket for letter
Cast on 10 stitches.
Stocking stitch 10 rows. Cast off leaving enough yarn to sew the pocket on to the planet.

Making up Planet a
Sew up the back seam allowing space for stuffing the planet. Sew up remaining gap. Sew the pocket on to the back side of the planet. Using two strands of double knitting wool, embroider the letter a on to the knitted planet. Cut out the felt tree and apples using the pattern template on page 74. Sew on to the planet using an overstitch.

> Size 4 needles
> Pinkish red or cerise double knitting wool

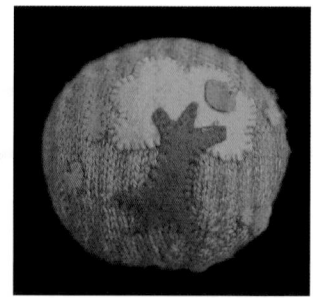

Action for Planet a:
Pretend to sneeze saying a, a, a, atishoo

Planet a can make you sneeze,
And all the apples blow off the trees.
a, a, a, atishoo

Baby bear

Bud the baby bear is not very big. Sometimes he wishes that he lived in a bungalow as he has problems climbing the stairs of his house. He can crawl up them on his hands and knees but has to b, b, b, bump on his bottom to get all the way downstairs.

Size 4 needles
Light brown double knitting wool

Knitting pattern to make the baby bear

Head
Cast on 6st
Row 1: Kfb to end of row (12 sts)
Row 2: P
Row 3: [Kfb, k1, kfb] repeat 4 times (20sts)
Row 4: P
Row 5: [Kfb, k3, kfb] repeat 4 times (28sts)
Row 6: P
Row 7:[Kfb, k5, kfb] repeat 4 times (36sts)
Row 8: P
Stocking st for 8 rows
Row 17: [K2tog, K5, skpo] 4 times (28sts)
Row 18: P
Row 19: [K2tog, K3, skpo] 4 times (20sts)
Row 20: P
Row 21: [K2tog, K1, skpo] 4 times (12sts)
Thread yarn through stitches and pull together

Nose
Cast on 20 sts
Row 1: k
Row 2: p
Row 3: k
Row 4: [p2tog] repeat to end of row
Thread yarn through stitches and pull together

Ears x2
Cast on 4 sts
Row 1: kfb, k2, kfb
Row 2: p
Row 3: kfb, k4, kfb
Row 4: p
Row 5: kfb, k6, kfb (10sts)
Row 6: p
Thread yarn through stitches and pull together

Body
Cast on 6 sts
Row 1: Kfb to end of row (12 sts)
Row 2: P

Row 3: [Kfb, k1, kfb] repeat 4 times (20sts)
Row 4: P
Row 5: [Kfb, k3, kfb] repeat 4 times (28sts)
Row 6: P
Row 7: [Kfb, k5, kfb] repeat 4 times (36sts)
Row 8: P
Row 9: [Kfb, k7, kfb] repeat 4 times (44sts)
Row 10: P
Stocking st for 8 rows
Row 19: [K2tog, K7, skpo] 4 times (36sts)
Row 20: P
Row 21: [K2tog, K5, skpo] 4 times (28sts)
Row 22: P
Row 23: [K2tog, K3, skpo] 4 times (20sts)
Row 24: P
Row 25: [K2tog, K1, skpo] 4 times (12sts)
Thread yarn through stitches and pull together

Legs x2
Cast on 14 sts
Stocking st for 14 rows
Row 15: K6, Kfb, Kfb, K6,
Row 16: P
Row 17: K7, Kfb, Kfb, K7
Row 18: P
Row 19: K8, Kfb, Kfb, K8 (20sts)
Row 20: P
Row 21: k
Row 22: P
Row 23: [K2tog] rep to end of row
Thread yarn through sts and pull together

Arms x2
Start at the top of bear's arms
Cast on 6sts
Row 1: Kfb in all stitches (12sts)
Row 2: P
Stocking st for 20 rows
Thread yarn through sts and pull together

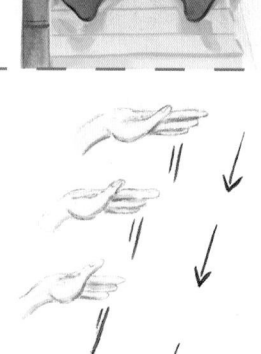

Action for the baby bear: Start with your hand up high and pretend it is bouncing down stairs saying b, b, b

Making up
Head and body: Sew from each end of the head leaving gap in the middle to stuff. Fill with stuffing. Sew up gap. Do the same with the body and sew the head on to the body.

Nose: Sew up the seam starting from the tip of nose. Loosely fill with stuffing. Don't put too much stuffing in or the nose will look too big. Stitch the nose on to the front of head.

Ears: Stitch the ears to each side of the teddy bear head using the shaping at the top of the head to position them.

Arms: Sew from the hand to under arm. Fill with stuffing. Position the arms to each side of the body and sew on.

Legs: Sew from heel to top of leg. Fill with stuffing. Position legs to the base of body and sew them on.

Finishing off
Embroider nose, mouth and eyes using brown wool. Using the templates on page 75 cut out two felt feet pads, two paw pads and two (optional) ear linings. Position correctly and sew on using overstitch. Sew a pocket on to the back side of the bear (using the same pattern as shown for Planet a). Using two strands of double knitting wool, embroider the letter b on to the bear.

Baby bear likes to run and jump. He dashes downstairs with a bump, bump, bump. b, b, b bump

Clicking cat

Con the clicking cat has always enjoyed taking photos with her camera.
You know she's coming when you hear her camera going c, c, c, click.

Size 4 needles
Cream and black double knitting wool

Knitting pattern to make clicking cat

Head and body
Starting at nose
Cast on 6st in cream
Row 1: [Kfb] 5 times, K1 (11sts)
Row 2: p
Row 3: [Kfb] 10 times, K1 (21sts)
Row 4: p
Row 5: K2, [Kfb, K4] 3 times, Kfb, K3 (25sts)
Row 6: P
Row 7: K2, Kfb, K6, Kfb, K4, Kfb, K6, Kfb, K3 (29sts)
Row 8: P
Row 9: K2, Kfb, K8, Kfb, K4, Kfb, K8, Kfb, K3 (33sts)
Row 10: P
Row 11: K2, Kfb, K10, Kfb, K4, Kfb, K10, Kfb, K3 (37sts)
Row 12: P
Row 13: K2, Kfb, K12, Kfb, K4, Kfb, K12, Kfb, K3 (41sts)
Row 14: P
Row 15: K
Row 16: P
Row 17: K2, skpo, K12, skpo, K5, K2tog, K12, K2tog, K2 (37sts)
Row 18: P
Row 19: K2, skpo, K10, skpo, K5, K2tog, K10, K2tog, K2 (33sts)
Row 20: P
Row 21: K2, skpo, K8, skpo, K5, K2tog, K8, K2tog, K2 (29sts)
Row 22: P
Row 23: K
Row 24: P
You are now starting the cat's body
Row 25: K1, [Kfb, K1] rep to end of row (43 sts)
Row 26: P
Continue in stocking st for 24 rows.
Row 51: K1 [K2tog, K1] rep to end of row
Row 52: P
Row 53: K1 [K2tog] rep to end of row (15 sts)
Row 54: P

Thread yarn through remaining 15 sts and pull together to form cat's bottom.
Keep a length of thread to sew the cat up.

First ear
Cast on 3sts in cream
Row 1: kfb, kfb, k1
Row 2: p
Row 3: k1, kfb, kfb, k2
Row 4: p
Row 5: k2, kfb, kfb, k3 (9sts)
Row 6: p
Cast off

Second ear
Cast on 3sts in cream
Row 1: kfb, kfb, k1
Row 2: p
Row 3: k1, kfb, kfb, k2
Row 4: p
Change to black wool
Row 5: k2, kfb, kfb, k3
Row 6: p
Cast off

Legs x 3
Cast on 15 sts in cream
Stocking st for 10 rows
Row 11: K6, Kfb, Kfb, K7 (17sts)
Row 12: P
Row 13: K7, Kfb, Kfb, K8 (19sts)
Row 14: P
Row 15: K8, Kfb, Kfb, K9 (21sts)
Row 16: P
Row 17: K2tog, K17, K2tog (19sts)
Row 18: p
Row 19: [k1, K2tog] rep to last st, k1
Row 20: P
Row 21: [K2tog] rep to last st, k1
Thread yarn through sts and pull together
For the 4th leg change to black yarn from row 17

Tail

Cast on 10sts in cream
Stocking stitch for 20 rows
Change to black
Row 21: [k1, k2tog] rep to last st, k1
Row 22: p
Row 23: k
Row 24: p
Thread yarn through sts and pull together

Making up

Head and body: Sew from each end of the head and body leaving a gap in the middle. Fill with stuffing. Sew up the gap.

Ears: Stitch the ears to each side of the cat's head using the shaping at the top of the head to position them.

Legs: Sew from heel to top of leg. Fill with stuffing. Position legs to the base of body and sew them on tightly.

Tail: Neatly stitch the sides together stuffing the tail as you go. Sew the tail to the rear of the cat so that it sticks up in the air.

Finishing off

Embroider mouth and eyes using black wool. Add whiskers by sewing in a few threads of black wool and separating the strands.

Sew a pocket on to the back side of the cat (using the same pattern as shown in planet a). Using two strands of double knitting wool, embroider the letter c onto the cat.

Camera

Cast on 10sts in grey
Stocking stitch for 7 rows
Row 8: k (should be a purl row)
Row 9: k
Row 10: p
Row 11: k
Row 12: k (should be a purl row)
Row 13: k
Row 14: p
Stocking stitch for 5 rows
(k row, p row, k row, p row, k row)
Row 20: k (should be a purl row)
Row 21: k
Row 22: p
Row 23: k
Cast off

Clicking cat is very quick. She grabs her camera and starts to click. c, c, c, click

Making up camera

Sew the two ends together. The camera will fold along the ridges formed by the knit on purl row. Sew both side seams leaving a space to put in stuffing. Sew up gap. Make the front of the camera from black and white felt using the template on page 76. Use a popper to attach to clicking cat's paw.

Dancing dinosaur

Deb the dinosaur just can't stop dancing.
Sometimes she d, d, dances from dusk until dawn.

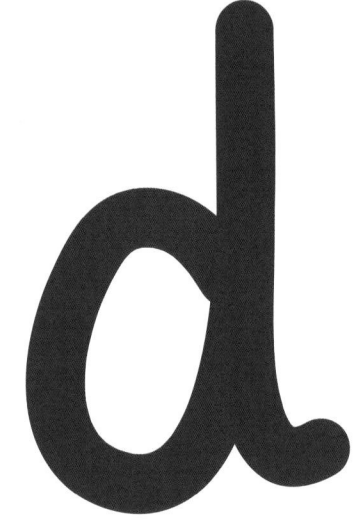

Size 4
needles
Dark green
double knitting
wool

Knitting pattern to make dancing dinosaur

Cast on 9 sts in dark green
Row 1: [kfb, k1] 4 times, k1 (13sts)
Row 2: p
Row 3: [kfb, k1, kfb] 4 times, k1 (21sts)
Row 4: p
Row 5: [kfb, k3, kfb] 4 times, k1 (29sts)
Row 6: p
Row 7: [kfb, k5, kfb] 4 times, k1 (37sts)
Row 8: p
Stocking st for 6 rows
Row 15: [k2tog, k5, skpo] 4 times, k1 (29sts)
Row 16: p
Row 17: [k2tog, k3, skpo] 4 times, k1 (21sts)
Row 18: p
Neck - stocking stitch for 8 rows
Row 27: [kfb, k3, kfb] 4 times, k1 (29sts)
Row 28: p
Row 29: [kfb, k5, kfb] 4 times, k1 (37sts)
Row 30: p
Row 31: [kfb, k7, kfb] 4 times, k1 (45sts)
Row 32: p
Row 33: [kfb, k9, kfb] 4 times, k1 (53sts)
Row 34: p
Row 35: [kfb, k11, kfb] 4 times, k1 (61sts)
Row 36: p
Stocking st for 8 rows
Row 45: [k2tog, k11, skpo] 4 times, k1 (53sts)
Row 46: p
Row 47: k
Row 48: p
Row 49: [k2tog, k9, skpo] 4 times, k1 (45sts)
Row 50: p
Row 51: k
Row 52: p
Row 53: [k2tog, k7, skpo] 4 times, k1 (37sts)
Row 54: p
Row 55: k
Row 56: p
Continue decreasing in this way until there are
13sts, then p, k, p the next three rows
Row 69: k
Row 70: p

Row 71: [k1, skpo] repeat to last st, k1 (9sts)
Thread yarn through sts and pull together

Legs x4
Cast on 16sts
Stocking stitch for 14 rows
Row 15: [k1, k2tog] repeat to last st, k1
Row 16: p
Row 17: [k2tog] repeat to last st, k1
Thread yarn through sts and pull together

Making up
Cut out triangles from thick red felt (using the
template on page 77) to form the spine of
dancing dinosaur.
Head and body: Sew the red triangles to one
side of the dinosaur's back using thin thread.
Sew together both sides of the dinosaur's back
and head leaving a small gap for stuffing. Fill
with stuffing. Sew up the gap making sure the
red triangles are firmly sewn in.
Legs: Sew from heel to top of leg. Fill with
stuffing. Position legs to the base of body and
sew them on tightly.

Finishing off
Embroider mouth using black wool. Cut circles
out of white felt (using the template on page 77).
Sew eyes on to the head using an overstitch.
Embroider a small dot in the centre of the
eye. Sew a pocket on to the back side of the
dinosaur (using the same pattern as shown in
planet a). Using two strands of double knitting
wool, embroider the letter d onto the dinosaur.

Action for dancing dinosaur
Dance your fingers on your
knees saying d, d, d

ancing dinosaur
stamps her feet.
She dances to
the steady beat.
d, d, d, dance

Planet e the exciting planet

Out in space, but not too far away, there is a planet – Planet e. Planet e is known as the exciting planet because so many interesting things happen there. Everything is so e, e, exciting.

Size 4 needles Green double knitting wool

Knitting pattern to make Planet e

Cast on 9 sts
Row 1: [kfb, k1] repeat x 4, k1 (13sts)
Row 2: p
Row 3: [kfb, k1, kfb] repeat x4, k1 (21sts)
Row 4: p
Row 5: [kfb, k3, kfb] repeat x4, k1 (29sts)
Row 6: p
Row 7: [kfb, k5, kfb] repeat x4, k1 (37sts)
Row 8: p
Row 9: [kfb, k7, kfb] repeat x4, k1 (45sts)
Row 10: p
Row 11: [kfb, k9, kfb] repeat x4, k1 (53sts)
Row 12: p
Row 13: [kfb, k11, kfb] repeat x4, k1 (61 sts)
Row 14: p
Row 15: [kfb, k13, kfb] repeat x4, k1 (69sts)
Row 16: p
Row 17: [kfb, k15, kfb] repeat x4, k1 (77 sts)
Row 18: p
Stocking stitch for 12 rows
Row 31: k1 [k2tog, k14, skpo, k1] repeat x4 (69sts)
Row 32: p
Row 33: k1 [k2tog, k12, skpo, k1] repeat x4 (61sts)
Row 34: p
Row 35: k1 [k2tog, k10, skpo, k1] repeat x4 (53sts)
Row 36: p
Row 37: k1 [k2tog, k8, skpo, k1] repeat x4 (45sts)
Row 38: p
Row 39: k1 [k2tog, k6, skpo, k1] repeat x4 (37sts)
Row 40: p
Row 41: k1 [k2tog, k4, skpo, k1] repeat x4 (29sts)
Row 42: p
Row 43: k1 [k2tog, k2, skpo, k1] repeat x4 (21sts)
Row 44: p
Row 45: k1 [k2tog, skpo, k1] repeat x4 (13sts)
Row 46: p
Thread yarn through stitches and pull tight.

Pocket for letter
Cast on 10 stitches
Stocking stitch 10 rows
Cast off leaving enough yarn to sew the pocket on to the planet

Making up Planet e
Sew up the back seam allowing space for stuffing the planet. Sew up remaining gap. Sew the pocket on to the back side of the planet. Using two strands of double knitting wool, embroider the letter e onto the knitted planet. Cut out the felt elephants and eggs using the pattern template on page 78. Sew on to the planet using an overstitch.

Action for Planet e:
Wave your arms in the air as if excited saying e, e, e

Planet e is very exciting.
There are coloured eggs
and elephants fighting.
e, e, e, exciting

Freezing frog

Where Fin the frog lives it is very, very cold. In fact it's freezing. Every morning Fin hops to his pond but quite often it's frozen over. The water's f, f, f, f freezing and so is Fin.

Knitting pattern to make freezing frog

Size 4 needles
Dark and light green double knitting wool

Head, body and legs
Cast on 9 sts in dark green
Row 1: [kfb, k1] 4 times, k1 (13sts)
Row 2: p
Row 3: [kfb, k1, kfb] 4 times, k1 (21sts)
Row 4: p
Row 5: [kfb, k3, kfb] 4 times, k1 (29sts)
Row 6: p
Row 7: [kfb, k5, kfb] 4 times, k1 (37sts)
Row 8: p
Row 9: [kfb, k7, kfb] 4 times, k1 (45sts)
Row 10: p
Stocking stitch for 6 rows
Row 17: [k2tog, k7, skpo] 4 times, k1 (37sts)
Row 18: p
Row 19: [k2tog, 5, skpo] 4 times, k1 (29sts)
Row 20: p
Row 21: k
Row 22: p
Row 23: [kfb, k5, kfb] 4 times, k1 (37sts)
Row 24: p
Start stripes – change to light green wool
Row 25: [kfb, k7, kfb] 4 times, k1 (45sts)
Row 26: p
Change to dark green wool (continue with dark and light green stripes every 2 rows)
Row 27: [kfb, k9, kfb] 4 times, k1 (53 st)
Row 28: p
Stocking stitch for 12 rows
Row 41: [k2tog, k9, skpo] 4 times, k1 (45sts)
Row 42: p
Row 43: [k2tog, k7, skpo] 4 times, k1 (37sts)
Row 44: p
Row 45: [k2tog, k5, skpo] 4 times, k1 (29sts)
Row 46: p
Row 47:k1 [k1, k2tog] rep to last st, k1 (20st)
Row 48: p

Legs
continuing on the remaining 20 sts and in 2 row stripes

Row 1: k 10 sts (turn - continue on these sts for right leg)
Row 2: p
Stocking stitch for 28 rows

Feet – in dark green only
Row 31: k 5 sts – fold sts in half so first 5 sts are facing second 5 sts
Using a third needle, knit together the first pair of sts, then the second and continue in this way to the end of the row (5 sts)
Row 32: p
Row 33: k1, kfb, kfb, k2
Row 34: p
Row 35: k2, kfb, kfb, k3
Row 36: p
Row 37: k3, kfb, kfb, k4
Row 38: p
Row 39: k4, kfb, kfb, k5 (13sts)
Row 40: p
Row 41: k4, skpo, k1, k2tog, k4
Row 42: p
Row 43: k3, skpo, k1, k2tog, k3
Row 44: p
Row 45: k2, skpo, k1, k2tog, k2
Row 46: p
Row 47: k1, skpo, k1, k2tog, k1
Cast off 5 stitches purlwise

Repeat leg and feet pattern on the remaining 10sts for left side

Arms x 2
Cast on 10 sts in dark green
Row 1: k
Row 2: p
Change to light green
Row 3: k
Row 4: p
Continue for 22 more rows in striped stocking stitch

Action for freezing frog:
Hug yourself wrapping hands round opposite shoulders saying f, f, f

Hands - in light green only

Row 27: k 5 sts – fold sts in half so first 5 sts are facing second 5 sts
Using a 3rd needle, knit together the first pair of sts, then the second and continue in this way to the end of the row (5 sts)
Row 28: p
Row 29: k1, kfb, kfb, k2
Row 30: p
Row 31: k2, kfb, kfb, k3
Row 32: p
Row 33: k3, kfb, kfb, k4
Row 34: p
Row 35: k3, skpo, k1, k2tog, k3
Row 36: p
Row 37: k2, skpo, k1, k2tog, k2
Row 38: p
Row 39: k1, skpo, k1, k2tog, k1
Cast off 5 stitches purlwise

Making up

Head, body and legs: Sew up from top of head to legs. Stuff the legs as you sew them up as they are thin. Fill the rest of frog with stuffing. With a few stitches, join at the seam to bend frog's legs at the knees.
Feet: Fold the feet in half and sew round the edges. With a few stitches sew frog's feet at the ankle end to his legs so they are bent at the ankle.
Arms: Sew up seam, stuffing as you go. Sew on to the body using shaping to position correctly.
Hands: Fold the hands in half and sew round the edges.

Finishing off

Embroider mouth using black wool. Cut circles out of white felt (using the template on page 79). Sew eyes on to the head using an overstitch. Embroider a small dot in the centre of each circle. Sew a pocket on to the back side of the planet (using the same pattern as shown in planet a). Using two strands of double knitting wool, embroider the letter f onto the frog.

Frog puts his feet into water that's ice. It's freezing cold and not very nice. f, f, f, freezing

Growling gorilla

Gus the growling gorilla lives in the jungle. He loves to growl. He says he is the king of the jungle and he thumps his chest and g, g, g, growls at anyone who comes near.

Size 4 needles
Black double knitting wool

Knitting pattern to make growling gorilla

Head, body and legs
Cast on 9 sts in black
Row 1: [kfb, k1] 4 times, k1 (13sts)
Row 2: p
Row 3: [kfb, k1, kfb] 4 times, k1 (21sts)
Row 4: p
Row 5: [kfb, k3, kfb] 4 times, k1 (29sts)
Row 6: p
Row 7: [kfb, k5, kfb] 4 times, k1 (37sts)
Row 8: p
Row 9: [kfb, k7, kfb] 4 times, k1 (45sts)
Row 10: p
Row 11: [kfb, k9, kfb] 4 times, k1 (53 sts)
Row 12: p
Stocking st for 8 rows
Row 21: [k2tog, k9, skpo] 4 times, k1 (45sts)
Row 22: p
Row 23: [k2tog, k7, skpo] 4 times, k1 (37sts)
Row 24: p
Row 25: k
Row 26: p
Row 27: [kfb, k7, kfb] 4 times, k1 (45sts)
Row 28: p
Row 29: [kfb, k9, kfb] 4 times, k1 (53sts)
Row 30: p
Row 31: [kfb, k11, kfb] 4 times, k1 (61 st)
Row 32: p
Stocking stitch for 16 rows
Row 49: [k2tog, k11, skpo] 4 times, k1 (53sts)
Row 50: p
Row 51: [k2tog, k9, skpo] 4 times, k1 (45sts)
Row 52: p
Row 53: [k2tog, k7, skpo] 4 times, k1 (37sts)
Row 54: p
Row 55: [k2tog, k5, skpo] 4 times, k1 (29sts)
Row 56: p
Legs – continuing on the remaining 29 sts
Row 1: k 13, k2tog (turn - continue on these 14sts for right leg)
Row 2: p
Stocking stich for 18 rows

Feet
Row 21: k6, kfb, kfb, k6 (16sts)
Row 22: p
Row 23: k7, kfb, kfb, k7
Row 24: p
Row 25: k8, kfb, kfb, k8
Row 26: p
Row 27: k2tog k16, k2tog
Row 28: p
Row 29: [k2tog] repeat to end of row
Thread yarn through remaining stitches and pull together
Repeat leg and feet pattern on the remaining 14sts for left side

Arms x 2
Cast on 14 sts
Stocking stitch for 30 rows
Row 31: [k2tog] repeat to end of row
Thread yarn through remaining stitches and pull together

Ears x2
Cast on 16 sts
Stocking stitch for 4 rows
Row 5: [k2tog] repeat to end of row
Thread yarn through remaining stitches and pull together

Making up
Head, body and legs: Sew up from top of head to legs leaving a gap for stuffing. It is easier to stuff the legs as you go. Fill with stuffing.
Arms: Sew from each end. Fill with stuffing. Sew on to the body using shaping to position correctly.
Ears: Fold each ear in half and sew along the seam and at the base of the ear. Pull the base in slightly. Sew on to the head using shaping to position correctly.

Action for growling gorilla: Thump your chest with you fists saying g, g, g

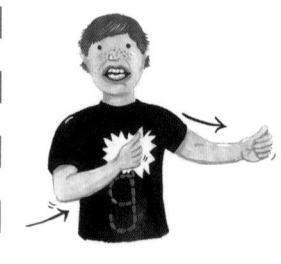

Growling gorilla
thumps his chest.
He growls at the
lions and says,
'I am the best'.
g, g, g, growl

Finishing off

Embroider mouth and nose using grey wool. Using grey wool, make big stitches to show toes on the gorilla's feet. Cut circles out of white felt (using the template on page 79). Sew eyes on to the head using an overstitch. Embroider a small dot in the centre of the eye. Sew a pocket on to the back side of the gorilla (using the same pattern as shown in planet a). Using two strands of double knitting wool, embroider the letter g onto the gorilla.

Huffing horse

Hal the huffing horse is always in a hurry. He hurries so much that he often gets very puffed out and he goes h, h, h, huff.

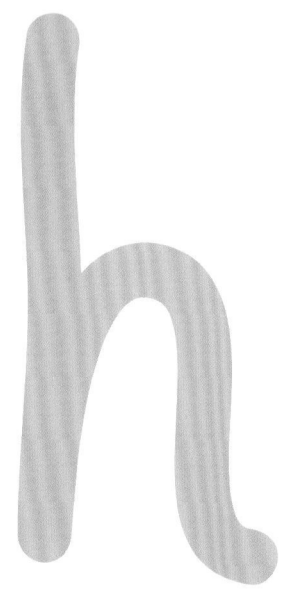

Knitting pattern to make huffing horse

Starting at nose
Cast on 4st
Row 1: [Kfb] 3 times, K1 (7sts)
Row 2: P
Row 3: [Kfb] 6 times, K1 (13sts)
Row 4: p
Row 5: K3, Kfb, K4, Kfb, K4 (15sts)
Row 6: P
Row 7: K4, Kfb, K4, Kfb, K5 (17sts)
Row 8: P
Row 9: K5, Kfb, K4, Kfb, K6 (19sts)
Row 10: P
Row 11: K6, Kfb, K4, Kfb, K7 (21sts)
Row 12: P
Row 13: K2, [Kfb, K4] 3 times, Kfb, K3 (25sts)
Row 14: P
Row 15: K2, Kfb, K6, Kfb, K4, Kfb, K6, Kfb, K3 (29sts)
Row 16: P
Row 17: K2, Kfb, K8, Kfb, K4, Kfb, K8, Kfb, K3 (33sts)
Row 18: P
Row 19: K2, Kfb, K10, Kfb, K4, Kfb, K10, Kfb, K3 (37sts)
Row 20: P
Row 21: K2, Kfb, K12, Kfb, K4, Kfb, K12, Kfb, K3 (41 sts)
Row 22: P
Row 23: K
Row 24: P
Row 25: K
Row 26: P (put a marker at each end of row)
Row 27: K2, skpo, K12, skpo, K5, K2tog, K12, K2tog, K2 (37sts)
Row 28: P
Row 29: K2, skpo, K10, skpo, K5, K2tog, K10, K2tog, K2 (33sts)
Row 30: P
Row 31: K2, skpo, K8, skpo, K5, K2tog, K8, K2tog, K2 (29sts)
Row 32: P
Row 33; K2, skpo, K6, skpo, K5, K2tog, K6, K2tog, K2 (25sts)
Row 34; P
Row 35; K2, skpo, K4, skpo, K5, K2tog, K4, K2tog, K2 (21sts)
Row 36' P
Row 37; K2, skpo, K2, skpo, K5, K2tog, K2, K2tog, K2 (17sts)
Row 38: P
Cast off

You are now starting the neck
Using the shaping of the horse's head pick up 30sts from the marker on the left side to the right side (15sts to the middle shaping and 15sts from the middle to the end). You are picking up across the back of the head.
Row 39: K
Row 40: P
Row 41: K
Row 42: P
Row 43: Kfb, k27, kfb, k1 (32sts)
Row 44: P
Row 45: K
Row 46: P
Start the back of the horse
Row 47: K21, turn
Row 48: P10, turn
Row 49: Sl1, K9
Row 50: Sl1, P9
Continue as for rows 49 and 50, on these 10 stitches for 24 rows. (hold stitches)
Cut off yarn and rejoin at the end of the first 11 sts.
Start the sides of the horse.
Row 75: (11 sts on needle) pick up and knit 14 sts from right side of horses back, k 10sts on needle, pick up 14sts from left side of horses back, k11sts on needle. (60sts)
Row 76: P
Stocking stitch for 4 rows
Row 81: Kfb, k57, kfb, k1
Row 82: P

Stocking stitch for 8 rows
Row 91: Kfb, k59, kfb, k1 (64sts)
Row 92: P
Row 93: k
Row 94: P
Row 95: K6, k2tog, k16, skpo, k12, k2tog, k16, skpo, k6 (60sts)
Row 96: P
Row 97: K6, k2tog, k14, skpo, k12, k2tog, k14, skpo, k6 (56sts)
Row 98: P
Row 99: k1, [k2tog] x5, k8, [skpo] x4, k2, [k2tog] x4, k8, [skpo] x5, k1 (38sts)
Row 100: P
Cast off

Legs x4
Cast on 4sts
Row 1: [Kfb] 3 times, K1 (7sts)
Row 2: P
Row 3: [Kfb] 6 times, K1 (13sts)
Row 4: p
Row 5: [Kfb, k2] 4 times, k1 (17sts)
Row 6: k (should be a purl row)
Continue in stocking stitch for 22 rows.
Cast off

Ears x2
Cast on 3sts
Row 1: Kfb, kfb, K1
Row 2: P

Row 3: k1, kfb, kfb, k2
Row 4: p
Row 5: k2, kfb, kfb, k3
Row 6: P
Row 7: k3, kfb, kfb, k4 (11sts)
Row 8: P
Cast off.

Tail
Using 6 strands of brown thread, plait (in twos) for 5cm. Leave a further 5cm for end of tail. Tie a knot at the end of the plaiting and fray out the wool at the end of the tail using a needle. This gives a frizzy appearance.

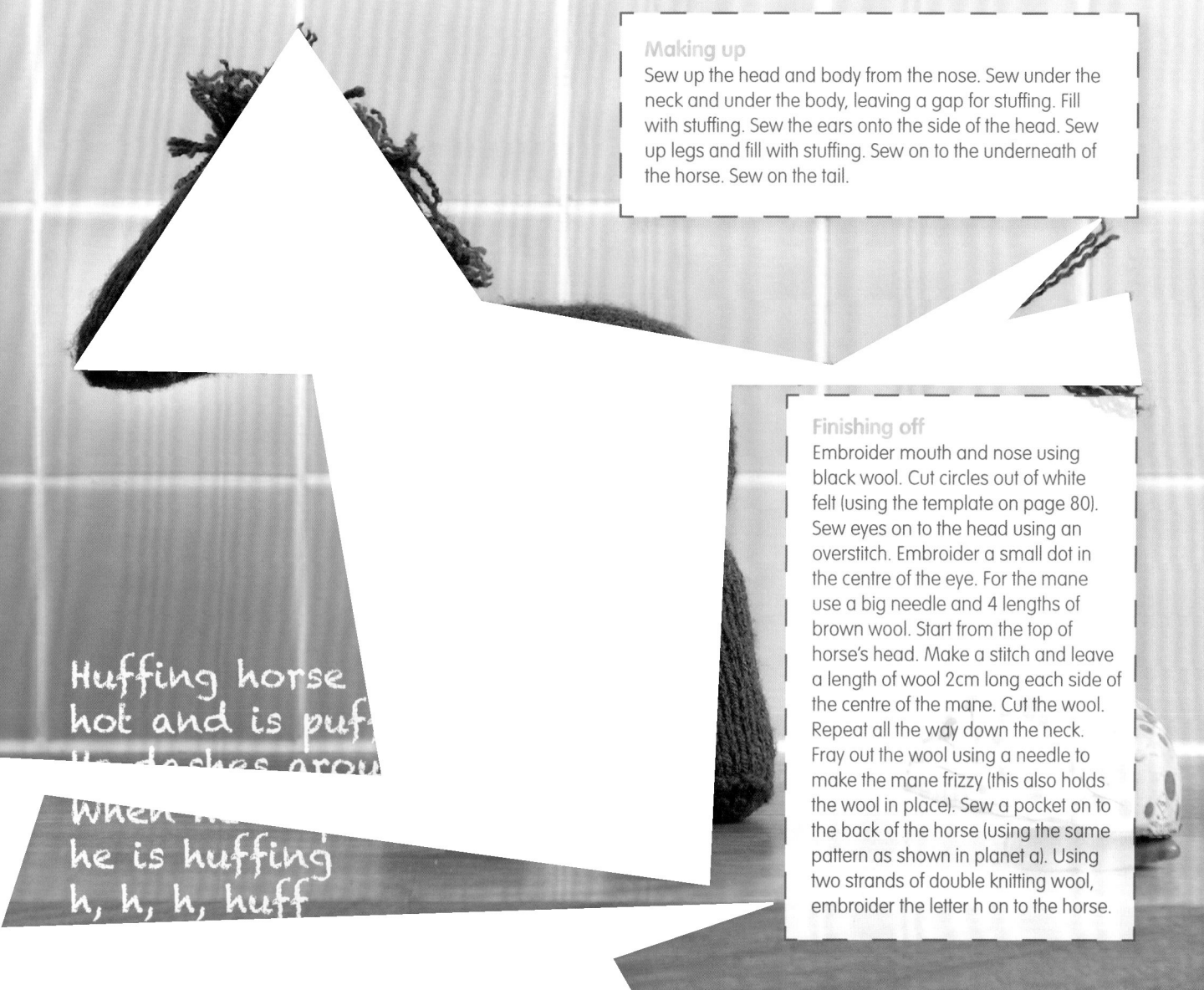

Making up
Sew up the head and body from the nose. Sew under the neck and under the body, leaving a gap for stuffing. Fill with stuffing. Sew the ears onto the side of the head. Sew up legs and fill with stuffing. Sew on to the underneath of the horse. Sew on the tail.

Finishing off
Embroider mouth and nose using black wool. Cut circles out of white felt (using the template on page 80). Sew eyes on to the head using an overstitch. Embroider a small dot in the centre of the eye. For the mane use a big needle and 4 lengths of brown wool. Start from the top of horse's head. Make a stitch and leave a length of wool 2cm long each side of the centre of the mane. Cut the wool. Repeat all the way down the neck. Fray out the wool using a needle to make the mane frizzy (this also holds the wool in place). Sew a pocket on to the back of the horse (using the same pattern as shown in planet a). Using two strands of double knitting wool, embroider the letter h on to the horse.

Huffing horse
hot and is puf
dashes arou
when
he is huffing
h, h, h, huff

Planet i – the itching planet

Out in space, but not too far away, there is a planet – Planet i.
It's not very nice living on Planet i; as soon as you land there you start to i, i, i, itch. In the end you have to jump off the planet to get away from all the itching.

Knitting pattern to make Planet i

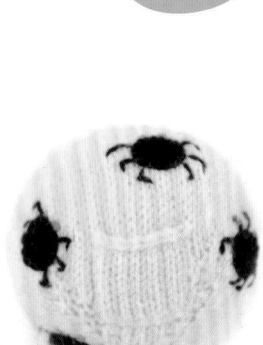

Size 4 needles
Pale yellow double knitting wool

Cast on 9 sts
Row 1: [kfb, k1] repeat x 4, k1 (13sts)
Row 2: p
Row 3: [kfb, k1, kfb] repeat x4, k1 (21sts)
Row 4: p
Row 5: [kfb, k3, kfb] repeat x4, k1 (29sts)
Row 6: p
Row 7: [kfb, k5, kfb] repeat x4, k1 (37sts)
Row 8: p
Row 9: [kfb, k7, kfb] repeat x4, k1 (45sts)
Row 10: p
Row 11: [kfb, k9, kfb] repeat x4, k1 (53sts)
Row 12: p
Row 13: [kfb, k11, kfb] repeat x4, k1 (61 sts)
Row 14: p
Row 15: [kfb, k13, kfb] repeat x4, k1 (69sts)
Row 16: p
Row 17: [kfb, k15, kfb] repeat x4, k1 (77 sts)
Row 18: p
Stocking stitch for 12 rows
Row 31: k1 [k2tog, k14, skpo, k1] repeat x4 (69sts)
Row 32: p
Row 33: k1 [k2tog, k12, skpo, k1] repeat x4 (61sts)
Row 34: p
Row 35: k1 [k2tog, k10, skpo, k1] repeat x4 (53sts)
Row 36: p
Row 37: k1 [k2tog, k8, skpo, k1] repeat x4 (45sts)
Row 38: p
Row 39: k1 [k2tog, k6, skpo, k1] repeat x4 (37sts)
Row 40: p
Row 41: k1 [k2tog, k4, skpo, k1] repeat x4 (29sts)
Row 42: p
Row 43: k1 [k2tog, k2, skpo, k1] repeat x4 (21sts)
Row 44: p
Row 45: k1 [k2tog, skpo, k1] repeat x4 (13sts)
Row 46: p
Thread yarn through stitches and pull tight.

Pocket for letter
Cast on 10 stitches
Stocking stitch 10 rows
Cast off leaving enough yarn to sew the pocket on to the planet

Making up Planet i
Sew up the back seam allowing space for stuffing the planet. Sew up remaining gap. Sew the pocket on to the back side of the planet. Using two strands of double knitting wool, embroider the letter i onto the knitted planet. Cut out seven black felt circles using the pattern template on page 80. Sew on to the planet using an overstitch. Embroider legs and eyes onto the insects.

Action for Planet i:
Scratch your arms with tips of fingers saying i, i, i

Planet i can make you itch.
You scratch and then jump in a ditch.
i, i, i, itch

Jumping Jack

Jumping Jack is a bit of a superhero. Ever since Jack was very, very small he loved to j, j, j, jump. One day he decided to take an extra big jump and jumped over his house. His jumping journeys have taken him over the moon and even up to the planets rescuing anyone in need. What a hero!

Size 4 needles Beige, red, blue and a small amount of black double knitting wool

Knitting pattern to make jumping Jack

Jack is made by knitting head, body and legs in one piece.

Head, body and legs

Head

Cast on 7 sts in beige
Row 1: [kfb] 6 times, k1 (13sts)
Row 2: p
Row 3: [kfb, k1, kfb] 4 times, k1 (21sts)
Row 4: p
Row 5: [kfb, k3, kfb] 4 times, k1 (29sts)
Row 6: p
Row 7: k6, kfb, kfb, k12, kfb, kfb, k7 (33sts)
Row 8: p
Stocking stitch for 10 rows
Row 19: k6, skpo, k2tog, k12, skpo, k2tog, k7 (29sts)
Row 20: p
Row 21:[k2tog, k3, skpo] 4 times, k1 (21sts)
Row 22: p
Row 23: k
Row 24: p

Body

Change to red
Row 25: [kfb] rep in all sts (42sts)
Row 26: p
Stocking stitch for 24 rows
Row 51: [K1, k2tog] repeat to the end of row (28sts)

Legs

Row 52: p
Row 53: k14, turn
Row 54: p
Stocking stitch on these 14sts for 38 rows
Change to black

Feet and shoes

Row 93: k6, kfb, kfb, k6
Row 94: p
Row 95: k7, kfb, kfb, k7
Row 96: p
Row 97: k8, kfb, kfb, k8 (20sts)
Row 98: p2tog. p16, p2tog
Row99: k2tog, k14, k2tog
Row 100: [p2tog] repeat
Thread yarn through remaining sts
Repeat on remaining 14sts for left leg

Arms x2

Cast on 12sts in red
Stocking stitch for 24 rows

Hands

Change to beige
Stocking stitch for 6 rows
Row 31: [k2tog] repeat
Thread yarn through remaining sts

Making up Jack

Body: The head, body and legs are knitted all in one. Sew down the back of the body and head and fill with stuffing. Sew down the back of the legs to the tips of the toes. Fill with stuffing as you go as the legs are thin.

Arms: Sew up the arm seams, filling with stuffing as you go. Sew the arms on to the body using the neck shaping to help with positioning. Sew each end of a popper to the hands to make them stay together.

Hair: Wrap double knitting yellow wool round a small book. The more wool you wrap, the thicker the hair. Carefully stitch over and under one side of the hair then back again so that every strand of hair is captured in the stitches. Cut the hair on the other side of the book so that there is an even amount of hair each side of the stitches. Position the hair at the top of the

Action for jumping Jack: Put your arms in the air as if you're a flying superhero saying j, j, j

Jack jumps so high and flies over the moon. He jumps over the planets but he'll be back soon. j, j, j, jump

head with the stitches in the centre. Spread the hair so that it runs down the side and back of Jack's head. Sew the hair tightly along the top of his head and round the bottom, back and sides of the head so that every strand of hair needs is sewn down. Cut the hair to the length you want it to be.

Face: Cut out small circles of white felt for the eyes. Sew eyes onto the face using brown thread and an overstitch. Embroider a small dot in the centre of the eye. Using the beige wool, pull up two stitches just below the centre of the eyes and pull tightly to create the nose. Using red wool, make two or three stitches just below the nose. This creates the mouth. Using the beige thread pull in a couple of stitches at the sides of Jack's head to create ears.

Jack's knickers
Cast on 42sts in blue double knitting yarn
Rib – k1, p1 for 4 rows
Stocking stitch for 8 rows
Row 13: [k1, k2tog] repeat to the end of the row
Row 14: p
Knicker leg
Row 15: k14, turn
Row 16: p (on 14sts)
Row 17: k
Row 18: k
Cast off.
Repeat on remaining 14sts for left leg

Jack's cloak
 starting at the bottom)
Cast on 30sts in blue
Knit for 4 rows
Row 5: k13, skpo, k2tog, k13 (28sts)

Row 6: p
Stocking stitch for 4 rows
Row 11: k12, skpo, k2tog, k12
Row 12: p
Stocking stitch for 4 rows
Row 17: k11, skpo, k2tog, k11
Row 18: p
Stocking stitch for 4 rows
Row 23: k10, skpo, k2tog, k10
Row 24: p
Stocking stitch for 4 rows
Row 29: k9, skpo, k2tog, k9
Row 30: k
Cloak ties
Row 31: cast on 20 sts, k20 (40sts)
Row 32: cast on 20 sts, k40 (60sts)
Row 33: k
Row 34: k
Row 35: k
Cast off

Sew a red pocket on to the back side of Jack's body (using the same pattern as shown in planet a). Using two strands of double knitting wool, embroider the letter j onto Jack's cloak. Cut a triangle out of yellow felt using the template on page 81. Stitch the triangle onto the front of Jack's chest. Using two strands of black double knitting wool, embroider the letter j on to the triangle.

Kicking kitten

Kev the kitten loves to k, k, k, kick balls and he is very good at it too. His Mum, Con the clicking cat, catches kicking kitten's tricks on her camera.

Size 4 needles Black double knitting wool and a small amount of cream

Knitting pattern to make kicking kitten

Head
Starting at nose
Cast on 6st in black
Row 1: [Kfb] 5 times, K1
Row 2: p
Row 3: [Kfb] 10 times, K1 (21sts)
Row 4: p
Row 5: K2, [Kfb, K4] 3 times, Kfb, K3 (25sts)
Row 6: P
Row 7: K2, Kfb, K6, Kfb, K4, Kfb, K6, Kfb, K3 (29sts)
Row 8: P
Row 9: K2, Kfb, K8, Kfb, K4, Kfb, K8, Kfb, K3 (33sts)
Row 10: P
Row 11: K
Row 12: P
Row 13: K2, skpo, K8, skpo, K5, K2tog, K8, K2tog, K2 (29 st)
Row 14: P
Row 15: K2, skpo, K6, skpo, K5, K2tog, K6, K2tog, K2 (25sts)
Row 16: P
Row 17: K
Row 18: P

Body
Row 19: K1, [Kfb, K1] rep to end of row (37sts)
Row 20: P
Continue in stocking st for 16 rows.
Row 37: K1 [K2tog, K1] rep to end of row
Row 38: P
Row 39: K1 [K2tog] rep to end of row
Row 40: P
Thread yarn through remaining stitches and pull together to form kitten's bottom.
Keep a length of thread to sew the kitten up.

First ear
Cast on 3sts in black
Row 1: kfb, kfb, k1
Row 2: p

Row 3: k1, kfb, kfb, k2
Row 4: p
Cast off
For the 2nd ear change to cream wool from row 3

Legs x 3
Cast on 13 sts in black
Stocking st for 8 rows
Row 9: K5, Kfb, Kfb, K6,
Row 10: P
Row 11: K6, Kfb, Kfb, K7
Row 12: P
Row 13: K7, Kfb, Kfb, K8
Row 14: P
Row 15: K2 tog, K15, K2tog,
Row 16: p
Row 17: [K2tog, k1] rep to last 2sts, k2tog
Row 18: P
Row 19: [K2tog] rep to last st, k1
Thread yarn through sts and pull together
For the 4th leg change to cream yarn from row 15

Tail
Cast on 9sts in black
Stocking stitch for 14 rows
Change to cream
Row 15: [k1, k2tog] rep to end
Row 16: p
Row 17: k
Row 18: p
Thread yarn through sts and pull together

Action for kicking kitten:
Use your index fingers on your lap to pretend to kick a ball saying k, k, k

Making up kicking kitten
Head and body: Sew from each end of the head and body leaving a gap in the middle. Fill with stuffing. Sew up the gap.
Ears: Stitch the ears to each side of the kitten's head using the shaping at the top of the head to position them.
Legs: Sew from heel to top of leg. Fill with stuffing. Position legs to the base of body and sew them on tightly.
Tail: Neatly stitch the sides together stuffing the tail as you go. Sew the tail to the rear of the kitten so that it sticks up in the air.

Finishing off

Embroider mouth and eyes using cream wool for the eyes and pink for the nose. Embroider a black dot in the centre of each eye. Add whiskers by sewing in a few threads of cream wool and separating the strands. Sew a pocket on to the back side of the kitten (using the same pattern as shown in planet a). Using two strands of double knitting wool, embroider the letter k on to the kitten.

Kitten's ball

Cast on 3sts in brown yarn
Row 1: [kfb] repeat 3 times
Row 2: p
Row 3: [kfb] repeat 6 times (12sts)
Row 4: p
Row 5: [kfb] repeat 12 times (24sts)
Row 6: p
Row 7: k
Row 8: p
Row 9: k
Row 10: p
Row 11: [k2tog] repeat 12 times
Row 12: p
Row 13: [k2tog] repeat 6 times
Row 14: p
Row 15: [k2tog] repeat 3 times
Thread yarn through sts
and pull together

Making up

Sew along the back seam leaving a gap for stuffing. Stuff the ball and sew up. Attach to kitten's foot using Velcro or a popper.

Kicking kitten knows all the tricks. He throws up the ball and flicks and kicks. k, k, k, kick

Licking Lion

Len the lion is extremely lazy. After he's woken up from a doze he likes to clean himself. He licks his paws – l, l, lick. He licks his face – l, l, lick. He licks his claws – l, l, lick. Then he lies down and goes back to sleep.

Size 4 needles
Beige double knitting wool, orange and brown for the mane and black for the whiskers

Knitting Pattern for licking lion

Licking lion is a puppet.
You need to knit 2 sides.
Cast on 6st in beige wool
Row 1: Kfb to end of row (12 sts)
Row 2: P
Row 3: Kfb, k4, kfb, kfb, k4, kfb (16sts)
Row 4: P
Row 5: Kfb, k6, kfb, kfb, k6, kfb (20sts)
Row 6: P
Row 7: Kfb, k8, kfb, kfb, k8, kfb (24sts)
Row 8: P
Stocking st for 18 rows
Arms
Row 27: Cast on 10sts, k to end of row
Row 28: Cast on 10sts, p to end of row (44sts)
Stocking stitch for 10 rows
Row 39: Cast off 8sts, k to end of row
Row 40: Cast off 8sts, p to end of row (28sts)
Stocking stitch for 20 rows
Row 61: k
Row 62: k
Repeat rows 61 and 62 twice more.
Cast off
Repeat for 2nd side.

Tail
Cast on 12sts in beige wool
Stocking stitch for 20 rows
Row 21: [k1, k2tog] rep to end of row
Row 22: p
Stocking stitch for 6 rows
Thread yarn through remaining stitches and pull together.

Making up the tail
Sew up the back seam and stuff the tail. Make a tassel out of the beige wool and sew it to the end of the tail.

Do not sew the two sides of the puppet together until you have finished embroidering the lion's features and sewn on the tail and pocket.

Finishing off and sewing up
Cut the nose out of black felt and the eyes out of white felt using the template on page 82. Sew the eyes and nose on to the lion's face using an over sewing stitch. Embroider a small dot in the centre of the eye. In brown yarn sew a couple of stitches in a line from the end of lion's nose and then stitch lion's mouth.

Add whiskers by sewing in a few threads of brown wool and separating the strands. Cut a tongue out of red felt using the template and sew it on to the mouth. In brown yarn use a running stitch to sew round the outside of lion's face – these stitches are for attaching the mane yarn. For the mane use four 30cm lengths of orange and brown yarn. Fold the four strands of yarn in half and using a thick needle or crochet hook attach the strands into each running stitch using a rug making knot. Do this all round the face, in each running stitch, to make a thick mane which can be trimmed. Use the picture of lion to help you sew the face and mane.

Sew a pocket on to the back side of the lion (using the same pattern as shown in planet a). Sew the tail on to the back of lion, just above the pocket. Using two strands of double knitting wool, embroider the letter l on to the front of lion. Neatly sew the back and front of the lion puppet together. Embroider claws on to lion's hands using brown yarn.

Action for licking lion: Pretend to lick your fingers and then wash your face with them saying l, l, l

Lazy lion licks his paws.
He cleans his face then
licks his paws.
l, l, l, lick

Munching monkey

Meg the monkey lives in the middle of the jungle.
Every morning she wakes up, grabs a banana and starts
to m, m, m, munch it.

Knitting pattern to make munching monkey

Head, body and legs
Cast on 9 sts in light brown
Row 1: [kfb, k1] 4 times, k1 (13sts)
Row 2: p
Row 3: [kfb, k1, kfb] 4 times, k1 (21sts)
Row 4: p
Row 5: [kfb, k3, kfb] 4 times, k1 (29sts)
Row 6: p
Row 7: [kfb, k5, kfb] 4 times, k1 (37sts)
Row 8: p
Row 9: [kfb, k7, kfb] 4 times, k1 (45sts)
Row 10: p
Stocking stitch for 6 rows
Row 17: [k2tog, k7, skpo] 4 times, k1 (37sts)
Row 18: p
Row 19: [k2tog, 5, skpo] 4 times, k1 (29sts)
Row 20: p
Row 21: k
Row 22: p
Row 23: [kfb, k5, kfb] 4 times, k1 (37sts)
Row 24: p
Row 25: [kfb, k7, kfb] 4 times, k1 (45sts)
Row 26: p
Row 27: [kfb, k9, kfb] 4 times, k1 (53 st)
Row 28: p
Stocking stitch for 12 rows
Row 41: [k2tog, k9, skpo] 4 times, k1 (45sts)
Row 42: p
Row 43: [k2tog, k7, skpo] 4 times, k1 (37sts)
Row 44: p
Row 45: [k2tog, k5, skpo] 4 times, k1 (29sts)
Row 46: p
Row 47:k1 [k1, k2tog] rep to last st, k1 (20 st)
Row 48: p

Legs – continuing on the remaining 20 sts
Row 49: k 10 sts (turn - continue on these sts for right leg)
Row 50: p
Stocking stitch for 28 rows

Feet
Row 79: k4, kfb, kfb, k4
Row 80: p
Row 81: k5, kfb, kfb, k5
Row 82: p
Row 83: k6, kfb, kfb, k6
Row 84: p
Row 85: k7, kfb, kfb, k7
Row 86: p
Row 87: k2tog to end of row
Thread yarn through remaining stitches and pull together
Repeat leg and feet pattern on the remaining 10sts for left side

Arms x 2
Cast on 10 sts in light brown
Stocking stitch for 30 rows
Thread yarn through remaining stitches and pull together

Ears x 2
Cast on 16 sts in light brown
Stocking stitch for 4 rows
Row 5: k2tog to end of row
Thread yarn through remaining stitches and pull together

Tail
Cast on 10sts
Stocking stitch for 30 rows
Row 31: [k1, k2tog] repeat to last stitch, k1
Row 32: p
Row 33: k
Row 34: p
Thread yarn through remaining stitches and pull together

Size 4 needles
Light brown double knitting wool (tweed or flecked yarn if you can find it)

Action for munching monkey: Pretend to peel a banana and munch it saying m, m, m

Making up

Head, body and legs: Sew up from top of head to legs leaving a gap for stuffing. It is easier to stuff the legs as you go. Fill with stuffing and sew up gap.

Arms and hands: Sew from each end leaving approx 3cm gap in the middle. Fill with stuffing. Sew on to the body using shaping to position correctly.

Ears: Fold ears in half and sew round the edges, slightly pulling in the side which you attach to the head. Sew on to the body using shaping to position correctly.

Tail: Sew from each end leaving approx 3cms gap in the middle. Fill with stuffing. Sew on to the back of the body.

Finishing off

Embroider mouth and nose using brown wool. Cut circles out of white felt (using the template on page 82). Sew eyes on to the head using an overstitch and embroider a dot in the centre of each circle. Cut a banana out of yellow felt using the template. Stitch the two sides of the banana together using brown cotton. In brown cotton embroider lines on to the banana. Sew the banana onto monkey's hand.

Sew a pocket on to the back side of the monkey (using the same pattern as shown in planet a). Using two strands of double knitting wool, embroider the letter m on to the monkey.

Munching monkey springs to her feet.

She grabs a banana and starts to eat. m, m, m, munch

Nodding nurse

Nat the nurse is always busy looking after her patients but she manages to keep herself neat and tidy in her nurse's uniform. Sometimes Nat is so busy dashing around the hospital that she hasn't time to answer questions with words. She just has to n, n, n, nod her head.

Knitting pattern to make nodding nurse

Nat is made by knitting head, body and legs in one piece.

Size 4 needles Beige double knitting wool and a small amount of black for shoes. Blue wool for dress and brown for hair

Head
Starting at top of head
Cast on 7 sts
Row 1: [kfb] 6 times, k1 (13sts)
Row 2: p
Row 3: [kfb, k1, kfb] 4 times, k1 (21sts)
Row 4: p
Row 5: [kfb, k3, kfb] 4 times, k1 (29sts)
Row 6: p
Row 7: k6, kfb, kfb, k12, kfb, kfb, k7 (33sts)
Row 8: p
Stocking stitch for 10 rows
Row 19: k6, skpo, k2tog, k12, skpo, k2tog, k7 (29sts)
Row 20: p
Row 21:[k2tog, k3, skpo] 4 times, k1 (21sts)
Row 22: p
Row 23: k
Row 24: p

Body
Row 25: [kfb] rep in all sts (42sts)
Row 26: p
Stocking stitch for 24 rows
Row 51: [k2tog] repeat to the end of row (21sts)

Legs
Row 52: p10, k2tog, p9 (hold left leg sts and continue on 10sts for right leg)
Stocking stitch on these 10sts for 40 rows
Change to black

Feet and shoes
Row 93: k4, kfb, kfb, k4
Row 94: p
Row 95: k5, kfb, kfb, k5
Row 96: p

Row 97: k6, kfb, kfb, k6
Row 98: p2tog. p12, p2tog
Row99: k2tog, k10, k2tog
Row 100: [p2tog] repeat
Thread yarn through remaining sts
Repeat on remaining 10sts for left leg

Arms x2
Cast on 10 sts
Stocking stitch for 30 rows
Row 31: [k2tog] repeat
Thread yarn through remaining sts

Making up nurse
Head, body and legs: Sew down the back of the body and head and fill with stuffing. Sew down the back of the legs to the tips of the toes. Fill with stuffing as you go as the legs are thin.
Arms: Sew up the arm seams, filling with stuffing as you go. Sew the arms on to the body using the neck shaping to help with positioning.
Hair: In brown wool make hair for nodding nurse using the same method as jumping Jack's.

Finishing off
Cut out small circles of white felt for the eyes. Stitch to the face using brown thread and an overstitch. Embroider a small dot in the centre of the eye.
Using the beige wool, pull up two stitches just below the centre of the eyes and pull tightly. This creates the nose. Using red wool, make two or three stitches just below the nose. This creates the mouth.

Action for nodding nurse: Nod your head saying n, n, n.

Nurse's clothes

Size 4 needles
Blue knitting wool

Dress x2

Cast on 30sts
Rows 1-4: k
Rows 5-8: stocking stitch
Row 9: k9, skpo, k8, k2tog, k9 (28sts)
Row 10: p
Stocking stitch 6 rows
Row 17: k9, skpo, k6, k2tog, k9
Row 18: p
Stocking stitch for 6 rows
Row 25: k9, skpo, k4, k2tog, k9
Row 26: p
Stocking stitch for 6 rows
Row 33: k9, skpo, k2, k2tog, k9 (22sts)
Row 34: p
Row 35: k
Row 36: p

Sleeves

Row 37: Cast on 12 sts – k to end of row
Row 38: Cast on 12 sts – p to end of row (46sts)
Stocking stitch for 6 rows
Row 45: k21, skpo, k2tog, k21
Row 46: p
Row 47: k
Row 48: p
Cast off

Making up clothes

Sew up seams. Leave a hole large enough to fit over nurse's head for her neck.

Apron: Cut the apron out of white felt using the template on page 83. Make the neck and waist straps out of strips of white felt and sew them on to the apron. Using two strands of double knitting wool, embroider the letter n on to the nurse.

Headband: Cut the headband out of white felt using the template. Sew on a length of elastic so that the band fits around nurses' head. Embroider a small red cross on to the front of the headband or sew the headband to nurse's head. Sew a pocket on to the back side of nurse's dress (using the same pattern as shown in planet a).

'Do I have to stay in bed?'
Nat the nurse just
nods her head.
n, n, n, nod

Planet o – the orange octopus planet

Out in space, but not too far away, there is a planet – Planet o. Planet o is very hot and very o, o, o, orange. The only creature that lives on Planet o is a very old octopus. He spreads out his eight long legs over the surface of the planet and wiggles them off and on so they don't get too hot.

Knitting pattern to make Planet o

Size 4 needles
Orange double knitting wool

Cast on 9 sts
Row 1: [kfb, k1] repeat x 4, k1 (13sts)
Row 2: p
Row 3: [kfb, k1, kfb] repeat x4, k1 (21sts)
Row 4: p
Row 5: [kfb, k3, kfb] repeat x4, k1 (29sts)
Row 6: p
Row 7: [kfb, k5, kfb] repeat x4, k1 (37sts)
Row 8: p
Row 9: [kfb, k7, kfb] repeat x4, k1 (45sts)
Row 10: p
Row 11: [kfb, k9, kfb] repeat x4, k1 (53sts)
Row 12: p
Row 13: [kfb, k11, kfb] repeat x4, k1 (61 sts)
Row 14: p
Row 15: [kfb, k13, kfb] repeat x4, k1 (69sts)
Row 16: p
Row 17: [kfb, k15, kfb] repeat x4, k1 (77 sts)
Row 18: p
Stocking stitch for 12 rows
Row 31: k1 [k2tog, k14, skpo, k1] repeat x4 (69sts)
Row 32: p
Row 33: k1 [k2tog, k12, skpo, k1] repeat x4 (61sts)
Row 34: p
Row 35: k1 [k2tog, k10, skpo, k1] repeat x4 (53sts)
Row 36: p
Row 37: k1 [k2tog, k8, skpo, k1] repeat x4 (45sts)
Row 38: p
Row 39: k1 [k2tog, k6, skpo, k1] repeat x4 (37sts)
Row 40: p
Row 41: k1 [k2tog, k4, skpo, k1] repeat x4 (29sts)
Row 42: p

Row 43: k1 [k2tog, k2, skpo, k1] repeat x4 (21sts)
Row 44: p
Row 45: k1 [k2tog, skpo, k1] repeat x4 (13sts)
Row 46: p
Thread yarn through stitches and pull tight.

Pocket for letter
Cast on 10 stitches
Stocking stitch 10 rows
Cast off leaving enough yarn to sew the pocket on to the planet

Making up Planet o
Sew up the back seam allowing space for stuffing the planet. Sew up remaining gap. Sew the pocket on to the back side of the planet. Using two strands of double knitting wool, embroider the letter o onto the knitted planet. Cut out the octopus in pink felt using the pattern template on page 84. Cut five spots out of different coloured felt and sew them on to the octopus. Cut out two eyes from black felt and sew them on to the octopus. Sew the octopus on to the planet using an overstitch.

> **Action for Planet o:**
> **Form your index fingers and thumbs into round shape saying o, o, o**

Planet o is orange and hot.
An octopus lives there covered in spots.
o, o, o, octopus

Popping pig

Pug the pig just loves eating. Sometimes he eats so much that he nearly goes p, p, p, pop.

Knitting pattern to make popping pig

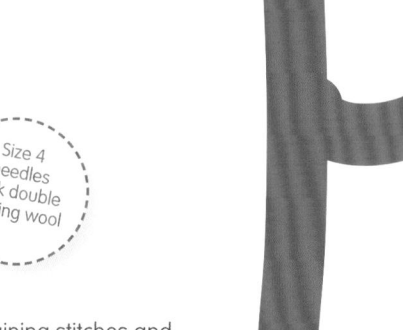

Size 4 needles Pink double knitting wool

Head and body
Starting at nose
Cast on 6st
Row 1: [Kfb] 5 times, K1 (11sts)
Row 2: p
Row 3: [Kfb] 10 times, K1 (21sts)
Row 4: k (should be a purl row)
Row 5: k
Row 6: p
Row 7: [Kfb, K3, Kfb] x4, k1 (29sts)
Row 8: P
Row 9: [Kfb, K5, Kfb] x4, k1 (37sts)
Row 10: P
Row 11: [Kfb, K7, Kfb] x4, k1 (45sts)
Row 12: P
Stocking stitch for 12 rows
Row 25: [k2tog, k7, skpo] x4, k1 (37sts)
Row 26: P
Row 27: [k2tog, k5, skpo] x4, k1 (29sts)
Row 28: P
Row 29: K
Row 30: P

Body
Row 31: [kfb] repeat to last st, k1 (57sts)
Row 32: p
Continue in stocking stitch for 30 rows.
Row 63: [K2tog, K1] rep to end of row
Row 64: P
Row 65: [K2tog] rep to end of row
Row 66: P
Thread yarn through remaining stitches and pull together to form pig's bottom.
Keep a length of thread to sew the pig up.

Ears x2
Cast on 3sts
Row 1: kfb, kfb, k1
Row 2: p
Row 3: k1, kfb, kfb, k2
Row 4: p
Row 5: k2, kfb, kfb, k3

Row 6: p
Row 7: k
Row 8: p
Thread yarn through remaining stitches and pull together

Legs x4
Cast on 4 sts
Row 1: Kfb in all stitches (8st)
Row 2: P
Row 3: Kfb in all stitches (16st)
Row 4: K (should be a purl row)
Row 5: K
Row 6: P
Stocking st for 12 rows
Cast off

Tail
Make a chain of 20sts using the crochet hook.

Making up pig
Head and body: Sew from each end of pig (his nose and bottom) leaving approximately a 3cm gap in the middle. Fill with stuffing. Sew up the gap.
Legs: Sew up from feet. Fill with stuffing. Sew to the underside of body.
Ears: Sew ears onto top of head using the shaping as a guide to position them evenly.
Tail: Sew the tail on to the centre of the pig's bottom. Twist the tail to make it curly and stitch into place.

Finishing off
Embroider eyes and nose using brown wool. Sew a pocket on to the side of the pig (using the same pattern as shown in planet a). Using two strands of double knitting wool, embroider the letter p on to the pig.

Action for popping pig:
Put your hands in front of you, palms facing and move your hands further and further away from each other saying p, p, p, pop. As you say pop, clap your hands.

Pug the pig just cannot stop.
He eats until he nearly goes pop.
P, P, P, pop

Quiet queen

Quin the quiet queen hates loud noises. One day quiet queen was looking through her telescope when she spotted Planet u. It looked so peaceful that she decided to travel there. Now she goes there all the time and sits q, q, q, quietly under her umbrella. She has to be very careful when Planet u turns upside down. She clings on tightly and holds on to her crown.

How to knit the quiet queen and her dress and crown

Use the same doll pattern for quiet queen as you used for nodding nurse, knitting it in brown yarn instead of beige. Then make her dress and crown using the patterns below. Use black wool for her hair and once it has been sewn on use a thick sewing needle to separate the strands of wool. This gives the hair volume.

Size 4 needles
Brown double knitting wool and a small amount of black for shoes and hair. Light and dark blue wool for dress

Quiet Queen's dress
Starting from front bib:
Cast on 12sts in light blue
Knit 4 rows
Row 5: p
Row 6: k12, cast on 10sts
Row 7: p22, cast on 10sts (32sts)
Row 8: k
Row 9: p
Row 10: k
Row 11: (dark blue) k
Row 12: k
Row 13: k
Row 14: k
Row 15: (light blue) k
Row 16: (kfb) repeat in all stitches (64sts)
Row 17: p
Stocking stitch for 39 rows
Row 57: (dark blue) k (this should be a purl row)
Row 58: k
Row 59: k
Row 60: k
Row 61: (light blue) k
Row 62: k
Cast off

Straps x2
In light blue cast on 3 sts
Stocking stitch for 16 rows.
Cast off.

Making up the dress
Sew up the back seam of the dress. Attach the straps to the front bib and back edge.

Crown
Cut the crown out of yellow felt using the template on page 85. Stitch up the back of the crown so that it fits round queen's head. In gold thread embroider the top of the crown using running stitch. You can use a small strip of Velcro or a popper to attach the crown to queen's head or sew the crown to quiet queen's head.

Sew a pocket on to the back of the queen's dress (using the same pattern as shown in planet a). Using two strands of double knitting wool, embroider the letter q onto the queen's dress.

Action for quiet queen:
Put your index finger up to your lips whispering q, q, q

Planet u is where quiet queen sits,
Under an umbrella where she neatly fits.
She has to be careful when it turns upside down.
Quiet queen quickly holds on to her crown.
q, q, q, quiet

Running robot

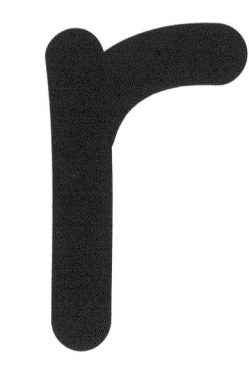

Rob the robot is always running and rushing around. But robot has to remember to plug himself in as he rests at night or the r, r, r of his motor gets slower and slower and then comes to a stop.

Knitting pattern to make running robot

Size 4 needles
Grey double knitting wool mixed with a fine silver thread (knit these 2 yarns together)

Head
Cast on 16sts
Stocking stitch for 15 rows
Row 16: k (should be a purl row)
Stocking stitch for 5 rows
Row 22: k (should be a purl row)
Stocking stitch for 15 rows
Row 38: k (should be a purl row)
Stocking stitch for 5 rows
Cast off

Head sides x2
Cast on 5sts
Stocking stitch for 15 rows
Cast off

Make up the head by sewing along the bottom seam and inserting the sides. Leave a gap to fill with stuffing then sew up.

Body and arms
Cast on 26sts
Row 1: k
Row 2: p5, k16, p5
Row 3: k
Row 4: p5, k16, p5
Row 5: k
Row 6: p5, k16, p5
Row 7: k
Row 8: k (should be a purl row)
Row 9: k
Row 10: p5, k16, p5
Row 11: k
Repeat rows 10 and 11 – 13 times (26 rows)
Row 38: k (should be a purl row)
Row 39: k
Row 40: p5, k16, p5
Row 41: k
Row 42: p5, k16, p5
Row 43: k
Row 44: p5, k16, p5

Row 45: k
Row 46: k (should be a purl row)
Row 47: k
Row 48: p5, k16, p5
Row 49: k
Repeat rows 48 and 49 – 13 times (26 rows)
Cast off

Body sides x2
Cast on 7sts
Stocking stitch for 27 rows
Cast off

Make up the body as for the head

Robot legs x2
Cast on 7 sts
Stocking stitch for 7 rows
Row 8: k (should be a purl row)
Stocking stitch for 27rows
Row 36: k (should be a purl row)
Stocking stitch for 7 rows
Row 44: k (should be a purl row)
Stocking stitch for 27 rows
Cast off

Leg sides x2 for each leg
Cast on 7sts
Stocking stitch for 27 rows
Cast off

Make up the legs as for the head

Action for running robot: Bend your arms at the elbow and move them backwards and forwards as if running saying r, r, r

Running robot
runs around
and around.
His motor makes
a rrring sound.
r, r, r, ring

Making up robot

Sew the head on to the top of the body (and arms). Sew the legs on to the base of the body. Using two strands of black double knitting wool use a running stitch to separate the arms from the body (the arms are the stocking stitched part and the body is the knitted part). Pull the stitches tight so you can see the difference between the arms and body.

Finishing off

Using the template on page 86 cut out the eyes in white felt. Sew them on to the robot using an overstitch. Using dark thread embroider a small cross in the middle of each eye. Using two strands of red double knitting wool embroider the mouth.

Sew a pocket on to the back of the robot's body (using the same pattern as shown in planet a). Using two strands of double knitting wool, embroider the letter r on to the front of robot.

Silly snake

Sid the snake is very, very silly. One day he saw his shadow and thought it was a stronger, scarier snake. He was so scared that he climbed into a tree and got s, s, s, stuck.

Knitting pattern to make silly snake

Starting from the tail
Cast on 3sts in green
Row 1: [kfb] repeat x3 (6sts)
Row 2: p
Row 3: k
Row 4: p
Row 5: [kfb] repeat x6 (12sts)
Row 6: p
Change to blue
Row 7: k
Row 8: p
Row 9: [kfb] repeat x12 (24sts)
Row 10: p
Row 11: k
Row 12: p
Change to green
Alternate green and blue stripes every 6 rows and continue in striped stocking stitch for 20 stripes. (120 rows)

Head
Row 133: k5, kfb, kfb, k10, kfb, kfb, k5 (28sts)
Row 134: p
Row 135: k6, kfb, kfb, k12, kfb, kfb, k6 (32sts)
Row 136: p
Row 137: k7, kfb, kfb, k14, kfb, kfb, k7 (36sts)
Row 138: p
Row 139 k8, kfb, kfb, k16, kfb, kfb, k8 (40sts)
Row 140: p
Row 141: k9, kfb, kfb, k18, kfb, kfb, k9 (44sts)
Row 142: p
Stocking stitch for 6 rows
Row 149: k9, skpo. K2tog, k18, skpo, k2tog, k9 (40sts)
Row 150: p
Row 151: k8, skpo. K2tog, k16, skpo, k2tog, k8 (36sts)
Row 152: p
Row 153: k7, skpo. K2tog, k14, skpo, k2tog, k7 (32sts)
Row 154: p

Row 155: k6, skpo. K2tog, k12, skpo, k2tog, k6 (28sts)
Row 156: p
Continue decreasing in this way until 20sts remain
Cast off

Tongue
Cast on 20sts in red
Knit 2 rows
Row 3: cast off 8sts, k to the end of row
Row 4: k12, cast on 8sts
Knit 2 rows
Cast off
(Alternatively you can make tongue in felt using the template on p87)

> Size 4 needles
> Green and blue double knitting wool and red for the tongue

Action for silly snake: Wiggle your hand up and down as if it is moving like a snake saying s, s, s

48

Silly snake
slithers into a tree.
He gets stuck
in the branches
and can't get free.
s, s, s, sssss

Making up
Sew up from the tail to the head leaving a gap for stuffing and a gap at the front of the head for the tongue. Sew the tongue firmly in to the space in the head. Fill with stuffing. Sew up gap. It may be easier to stuff snake as you sew up rather than leave it all to the end.

Finishing off
Cut out the eyes in red felt using the template on page 87. Sew them on to the snake's head using an overstitch. Embroider a black centre to each eye.

Sew a pocket on to the back side of the snake's head (using the same pattern as shown in planet a). Using two strands of double knitting wool, embroider the letter s on to the snake.

Ticking tiger

Tom the tiger is in a lot of trouble. One day when he was out hunting for food he heard a tick-tock coming from the hollow trunk of a tree. He grabbed the ticking thing and tucked it quickly into his mouth. Later, when he was tired he lay down to sleep and heard a tick-tock coming from his tummy. Now when he tries to roar the only sound that comes out is t, t, tick-tock.

Knitting pattern to make ticking tiger

The head and body are knitted in one piece

Head and body
Starting at nose
Cast on 6st in orange
Row 1: [Kfb] 5 times, K1 (11sts)
Row 2: p
Row 3: [Kfb] 10 times, K1 (21sts)
Row 4: p
Row 5: K2, [Kfb, K4] 3 times, Kfb, K3 (25sts)
Row 6: P
Row 7: K2, Kfb, K6, Kfb, K4, Kfb, K6, Kfb, K3 (29sts)
Row 8: P
Row 9: K2, Kfb, K8, Kfb, K4, Kfb, K8, Kfb, K3 (33sts)
Row 10: P
Row 11: K2, Kfb, K10, Kfb, K4, Kfb, K10, Kfb, K3 (37sts)
Row 12: P
Row 13: K2, Kfb, K12, Kfb, K4, Kfb, K12, Kfb, K3 (41sts)
Row 14: P
Row 15: K2, Kfb, K14, Kfb, K4, Kfb, K14, Kfb, K3 (45sts)
Row 16: P
Row 17: K
Row 18: P
Row 19: K2, skpo, K14, skpo, K5, K2tog, K14, K2tog, K2 (41sts)
Row 20: P
Row 21: K2, skpo, K12, skpo, K5, K2tog, K12, K2tog, K2 (37sts)
Row 22: P
Row 23: K2, skpo, K10, skpo, K5, K2tog, K10, K2tog, K2 (33sts)
Row 24: P
Row 25: K2, skpo, K8, skpo, K5, K2tog, K8, K2tog, K2 (29sts)

Row 26: P
Start stripes – alternate black and orange stripes every 4 rows
Row 27: K (black)
Row 28: P
Row 29: K1, [Kfb, K1] rep to end of row (43 sts)
Row 30: P
Change to orange (change colours every 4 rows)
Continue in stocking stitch for 34 rows.
Row 65: K1 [K2tog, K1] rep to end of row
Row 66: P
Row 67: K1 [K2tog] rep to end of row (15sts)
Row 68: P
Thread yarn through remaining 15sts and pull together to form tiger's bottom.
Keep a length of thread to sew the tiger up.

Ears x2
Cast on 3sts in black (orange and black stripes every 4 rows)
Row 1: kfb, kfb, k1
Row 2: p
Row 3: k1, kfb, kfb, k2 (orange)
Row 4: p
Row 5: k2, kfb, kfb, k3 (black)
Row 6: p
Row 7: k
Row 8: p
Cast off

Legs x 4
The orange and black stripes change every 4 rows. Cast on 17 sts in orange. Stocking st for 12 rows
Row 13: K7, Kfb, Kfb, K8,
Row 14: P
Row 15: K8, Kfb, Kfb, K9
Row 16: P

Size 4 needles
Orange and black double knitting wool

Action for ticking tiger:
Put your hands up in front of you and move them as if they are hands of a clock saying t, t, t

Ticking tiger
swallowed a clock.
Instead of roaring
he goes tick-tock.
t, t, t, tick-tock

Row 17: K9, Kfb, Kfb, K10
Row 18: P
Row 19: K2 tog, K19, K2tog,
Row 20: p
Row 21: [k1, K2tog] rep to last st
Row 22: P
Row 23: [K2tog] rep to end
Thread yarn through sts and pull together

Tail
Cast on 10sts in black (orange and black
stripes every 2 rows)
Stocking stitch for 24 rows
Change to black
Row 25: [k1, k2tog] rep to last st, k1
Row 26: p
Row 27: k
Row 28: p
Thread yarn through sts and pull together

Making up tiger
Head and body
Sew from each end of the head leaving a
gap in the middle. Fill with stuffing. Sew up
the gap.
Ears: Stitch the ears to each side of the
tiger's head using the shaping at the top of
the head to position them.
Legs: Sew from heel to top of leg. Fill with
stuffing. Position legs to the base of body
and sew them on tightly.
Tail: Neatly stitch the sides together stuffing
the tail as you go. Sew the tail to the rear of
the tiger.

Finishing off
Cut out a triangle of black felt for tiger's nose
and two circles of white felt for tiger's eyes
(using templates on page 87). Sew on to the
head using brown thread. Embroider a dot
in the centre of each eye circle. Embroider
mouth using black wool. Add whiskers by
sewing in a few threads of black wool and
separating the strands.

Sew a pocket on to the side of the tiger
(using the same pattern as shown in planet
a). Using two strands of double knitting
wool, embroider the letter t on to the tiger.

Planet u – the upside down planet

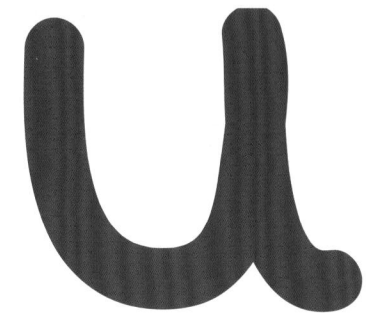

Out in space, but not too far away, there is a planet – Planet u.
Planet u is a very quiet place and it's the place where quiet queen likes to sit and think. The only trouble is that unfortunately every now and then it suddenly turns u, u, u, upside down and everything falls off.

Knitting pattern to make Planet u

Size 4 needles
Blue double knitting wool

Cast on 9 sts
Row 1: [kfb, k1] repeat x 4, k1 (13sts)
Row 2: p
Row 3: [kfb, k1, kfb] repeat x4, k1 (21sts)
Row 4: p
Row 5: [kfb, k3, kfb] repeat x4, k1 (29sts)
Row 6: p
Row 7: [kfb, k5, kfb] repeat x4, k1 (37sts)
Row 8: p
Row 9: [kfb, k7, kfb] repeat x4, k1 (45sts)
Row 10: p
Row 11: [kfb, k9, kfb] repeat x4, k1 (53sts)
Row 12: p
Row 13: [kfb, k11, kfb] repeat x4, k1 (61 sts)
Row 14: p
Row 15: [kfb, k13, kfb] repeat x4, k1 (69sts)
Row 16: p
Row 17: [kfb, k15, kfb] repeat x4, k1 (77 sts)
Row 18: p
Stocking stitch for 12 rows
Row 31: k1 [k2tog, k14, skpo, k1] repeat x4 (69sts)
Row 32: p
Row 33: k1 [k2tog, k12, skpo, k1] repeat x4 (61sts)
Row 34: p
Row 35: k1 [k2tog, k10, skpo, k1] repeat x4 (53sts)
Row 36: p
Row 37: k1 [k2tog, k8, skpo, k1] repeat x4 (45sts)
Row 38: p
Row 39: k1 [k2tog, k6, skpo, k1] repeat x4 (37sts)
Row 40: p
Row 41: k1 [k2tog, k4, skpo, k1] repeat x4 (29sts)
Row 42: p
Row 43: k1 [k2tog, k2, skpo, k1] repeat x4 (21sts)
Row 44: p
Row 45: k1 [k2tog, skpo, k1] repeat x4 (13sts)
Row 46: p

Thread yarn through stitches and pull tight.

Pocket for letter
Cast on 10 stitches. Stocking stitch 10 rows. Cast off leaving enough yarn to sew the pocket on to the planet.

Making up Planet u
Sew up the back seam allowing space for stuffing the planet. Sew up remaining gap. Sew the pocket on to the back side of the planet. Using two strands of double knitting wool, embroider the letter u on to the knitted planet. Cut out the umbrella in red felt using the pattern template on page 88. Sew on to the planet using an overstitch. Embroider the handle of the umbrella.

Attach a small piece of Velcro to the top of the umbrella on the planet and to the back of quiet queen's head so that she can stay there showing the q and the u together. Alternatively, knit a rectangle (8sts x 7rows) from black wool and attach to the top of the umbrella. Attach one end of a popper to this flap and the other end to the back of queen's dress.

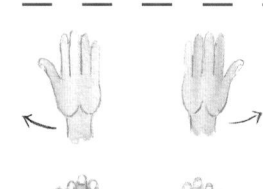
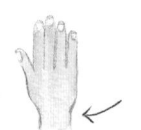

Action for Planet u:
Looking at hands from above, put your hand out in front of you, palm facing up and turn it over saying u, u, u

u, u, u, upside down

Land with a thump.

Planet u can make you jump.

It turns upside down and you

Val the vet - v

Val is a very, very good vet and she loves her job. She v, v, vrooms about in her van visiting sick animals and always helps them to get better.

How to knit Val the vet and her clothes

Use the same doll pattern for Val the vet as you used for nodding nurse. Use orange wool for her hair and add a fringe once the hair has been sewn on.

Size 4 needles Beige double knitting wool, green for clothes and orange for hair

Knitting patterns to make Val the vet's clothes

T-shirt x2
Cast on 30sts in green
Rows 1-4: k
Rows 5-8: stocking stitch
Row 9: k9, skpo, k8, k2tog, k9 (28sts)
Row 10: p
Stocking stitch for 6 rows
Row 17: k9, skpo, k6, k2tog, k9 (26sts)
Row 18: p
Row 19: k
Row 20: p

Sleeves
Row 21: Cast on 8 sts – k to end of row
Row 22: Cast on 8 sts – p to end of row (42sts)
Stocking stitch for 6 rows
Row 29: k19, skpo, k2tog, k19
Row 30: p
Stocking stitch 4 rows
Cast off

Making up
Sew up seams. Leave a hole large enough to fit over Val's head for her neck.

Trousers
Cast on 42sts in green
Rib – k1, p1 for 4 rows
Stocking stitch for 8 rows
Row 13: [k1, k2tog] repeat to the end of the row
Row 14: p
Trouser leg
Row 15: k14, turn
Stocking stitch for 35 rows
Row 51: k
Row 52: k
Row 53: k

Cast off.
Repeat on remaining 14sts for left leg

Making up
Sew up each leg and down the back seam.

Head band
Cut the headband out of white felt using the template on page 88. Embroider 'vet' in green on to the front of the band. Attach elastic to each side of the band making sure it fits snugly round Val's head or sew it on to Val's head.

Finishing Off
Sew the pocket on to the back side of Val the vet's t-shirt (using the same pattern as shown in planet a). Using two strands of double knitting wool, embroider the letter v on to the front of Val's t-shirt.

Action for Val the vet: Pretend to be turning the wheels on a van saying v, v, v

Val is visiting voles and bats. Her van is full of vipers and cats. She vrooms along the country roads. Then vrooms back home with a van full of toads.
v, v, v, vroom

Wild witch - w

Win the witch lives in a little cottage in the woods. She is called wild witch because she has wild hair, wild eyes and a wild, wild screechy voice. She just loves w, w, w, waving her wand.

How to knit wild witch and her clothes

Size 4 needles Green and black double knitting wool

Use the same doll pattern for wild witch as you used for nodding nurse except that she is knitted in green wool. When you get to her legs stocking stitch 2 rows green and 2 rows black so that she has striped legs. (Witch doesn't need shoes so continue with stripes along her feet). Use black wool for her hair and once it has been sewn on use a thick sewing needle to separate the strands of wool. This gives the hair volume.

Nose
Wild witch has a nose that is added to her face.
Cast on 7sts in green
Row 1: k
Row 2: p
Row 3: k2tog, k3, k2tog
Row 4: p
Row 5: k2tog, k1, k2tog
Row 6: p
Row 7: k3tog

Making up
Sew on to the middle of witch's face leaving a small gap to stuff. Fill with stuffing and sew up the gap.

Witch's clothes
Dress x2
Size 4 needles
Black double knitting wool
Cast on 30sts
Rows 1-4: k
Stocking stitch 6 rows
Row 11: k9, skpo, k8, k2tog, k9
Row 12: p
Stocking stitch 8 rows
Row 21: k9, skpo, k6, k2tog, k9
Row 22: p
Stocking stitch for 8 rows
Row 31: k9, skpo, k4, k2tog, k9

Row 32: p
Stocking stitch for 8 rows
Row 41: k9, skpo, k2, k2tog, k9
Row 42: p
Sleeves
Row 43: Cast on 12 sts – k to end of row
Row 44: Cast on 12 sts – p to end of row
Stocking stitch for 6 rows
Row 51: k21, skpo, k2tog, k21
Row 52: p
Row 53: k
Row 54: p
Cast off

Making up
Sew up seams. Leave a hole large enough to fit over witch's head for her neck.

Hat
Cut the hat out of black felt using the template on page 89. Sew the rim of the hat to the pointed part. (You can stuff this to make it more rigid). Put the top part of a popper on the bottom of the hat and the bottom part of a popper to witch's hair so that the hat stays on her head but can be taken off. Alternatively use black Velcro to attach the hat to witch's head.

Finishing off
Make a wand out of orange felt using the template. Sew it to witch's hand.

Sew the pocket on to the back side of wild witch's dress (using the same pattern as shown in planet a). Using two strands of double knitting wool, embroider the letter w on to the front of wild witch's dress.

Wild witch
waves her wand,
and all of the
frogs jump out
of the pond.
w, w, w, wave

Alien x

Alien x loves visiting places but his spaceship is getting very old. One day he jumped into the spaceship but when he pressed the button to make the engine start all that happened was an x, x, x noise. "Oh no!" said Alien x. "Now I'm going to have to get a new spaceship."

Knitting pattern for Alien x

Size 4 needles
Turquoise double knitting wool.

Alien x is a puppet. You need to knit two sides.

Use the same knitting pattern for Alien x as you used for licking lion but use a turquoise kniting yarn. Remember though not to sew up the sides of the puppet until you have finished embroidering him.

Finishing off
Cut out the eyes, mouth and spots from felt using the template on page 90. Stitch them on to the alien using an over sewing stitch (use the picture to help you).

Sew the pocket on to the back side of Alien x (using the same pattern as shown in planet a). Using two strands of double knitting wool, embroider the letter x onto the front of Alien x.

Cut Alien x's hair and hands out of green felt using the template. Cut two of each shape and sew each pair together around the edges using small stitches. This makes the hair and hands more rigid. Sew the hair on to one side of the puppet using thin thread. Do the same with the hands. Sew together the two sides so that the hair and hands are sandwiched between them.

Action for Alien x:
Pretend to push a rocket starter button with your finger saying x, x, x, x

The rocket of
alien x won't start.
It goes x, x, x.
It needs a new part.
x, x, x, x.

Yawning Yasmin

Yas loves playing with her yo-yo. The trouble is that once she starts yo-yoing she doesn't stop. She has been known to play on her yo-yo all through the night. She gets so tired that she can't stop y, y, yawning.

How to knit yawning Yasmin and her clothes

Use the same doll pattern for yawning Yasmin as you used for nodding nurse except that she is knitted in light brown wool. Yawning Yasmin has striped legs. Stocking stitch two rows white and two rows yellow when you get to her legs. (Yasmin doesn't need shoes so continue with stripes along her feet)

Use dark brown wool for her hair and make sure it is long enough to plait. (Use a bigger book than for jumping Jack to wrap the wool around) Once it has been sewn on, plait each side and tie with yellow thread.

Yawning Yasmin's dress
To make Yasmin's dress use the same pattern as quiet queen's dress but knit the main colour in pale yellow yarn and the second colour in bright yellow. Decrease the number of rows in the skirt of the dress by 10 so it is slightly shorter.

Size 4 needles
Light brown double knitting wool, pale yellow and bright yellow for dress and brown for hair

Finishing off
Make a yo-yo out of red felt using the template on page 91. Attach the yo-yo to a string and sew it to Yasmin's hand.
Sew the pocket on to the back side of yawning Yasmin's dress (using the same pattern as shown in planet a). Using two strands of double knitting wool, embroider the letter y on to the front of Yasmin's dress.

Yasmin's tired and starts to yawn. She's been up playing yo-yo from dusk until dawn. y, y, y, yawn

Action for yawning Yasmin:
Put your hand in front of your mouth as if yawning saying y, y, y

Zooming zebra

Zip the zooming zebra used to live in a zoo but one day the zoo keeper forgot to lock the gate and Zip z, z, zoomed out of the zoo.

Size 4 needles
Black and white double knitting wool

Knitting pattern to make zooming zebra

Starting at nose
Cast on 4st in black
Row 1: [Kfb] 3 times, K1 (7sts)
Row 2: P
Row 3: [Kfb] 6 times, K1 (13sts)
Row 4: p
Change to white
Row 5: K3, Kfb, K4, Kfb, K4 (15sts)
Row 6: P
Row 7: K4, Kfb, K4, Kfb, K5 (17sts)
Row 8: P
Change to black
Row 9: K5, Kfb, K4, Kfb, K6 (19sts)
Row 10: P
Row 11: K6, Kfb, K4, Kfb, K7 (21sts)
Row 12: P
Change to white
Row 13: K2, [Kfb, K4] 3 times, Kfb, K3 (25sts)
Row 14: P
Row 15: K2, Kfb, K6, Kfb, K4, Kfb, K6, Kfb, K3 (29sts)
Row 16: P
Change to black
Row 17: K2, Kfb, K8, Kfb, K4, Kfb, K8, Kfb, K3 (33sts)
Row 18: P
Row 19: K2, Kfb, K10, Kfb, K4, Kfb, K10, Kfb, K3 (37sts)
Row 20: P
Change to white
Row 21: K
Row 22: P
Row 23: K
Row 24: P (put in marker at end of each row)
Change to black
Row 25: K2, skpo, K10, skpo, K5, K2tog, K10, K2tog, K2 (33sts)
Row 26: P
Row 27: K2, skpo, K8, skpo, K5, K2tog, K8, K2tog, K2 (29sts)
Row 28: P
Change to white

Row 29: K2, skpo, K6, skpo, K5, K2tog, K6, K2tog, K2 (25sts)
Row 30: P
Row 31: K2, skpo, K4, skpo, K5, K2tog, K4, K2tog, K2 (21sts)
Row 32: P
Change to black
Row 33: K2, skpo, K2, skpo, K5, K2tog, K2, K2tog, K2 (17sts)
Row 34: P
Row 35: K
Row 36: P
Cast off

You are now starting the neck
In white, using the shaping of the zebra's head, pick up 30sts from the marker on the left side to the right side (15sts to the middle shaping and 15sts from the middle to the marker at the end) You are picking up across the back of the head.
Row 37: K
Row 38: P
Row 39: K
Row 40: P
Change to black
Row 41: Kfb, k27,kfb, k1
Row 42: P
Row 43: K
Row 44: P
Start the back of the zebra
Start with white and change from black to white every 4 rows
Row 45: K21, turn
Row 46: P10, turn
Row 47: Sl1, K9
Row 48: Sl1, P9
Continue as for rows 45 - 48 on these 10 stitches for 20 rows in stripes (hold stitches) Cut off yarn and rejoin at the end of the first 11sts.

Action for zooming zebra:
Make a z with your finger (left to right, diagonally across and right to left) with your finger saying z, z, z

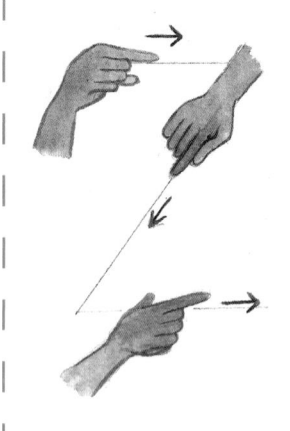

62

Start the sides of the zebra

Row 69: (11sts on needle) in white pick up and knit 14sts from right side of zebra's back, k 10sts on needle, pick up 14sts from left side of zebra's back, k11sts on needle. (60sts)

Row 70: P

Row 71: K

Row 72: P

Change to black

Row 73: Kfb, k57, kfb, k1

Row 74: P

Stocking stitch for 6 rows (changing to white after 2 rows)

Change to black

Row 81: Kfb, k59, kfb, k1 (64sts)

Row 82: P

Row 83: k

Row 84: P

Change to white

Row 85: K6, k2tog, k16, skpo, k12, k2tog, k16, skpo, k6 (60sts)

Row 86: P

Row 87: K6, k2tog, k14, skpo, k12, k2tog, k14, skpo, k6 (56sts)

Row 88: P

Change to black

Row 89: k1, [k2tog] x5, k8, [skpo] x4, k2, [k2tog] x4, k8, [skpo] x5, k1 (38 sts)

Row 90: P

Cast off

Legs x4

Cast on 4sts in black

Row 1: [Kfb] 3 times, K1

Row 2: P

Row 3: [Kfb] 6 times, K1

Row 4: p

Change to white

Row 5: K3, kfb, k4, kfb, k4 (15sts)

Row 6: k (should be a purl row)

Continue in stocking stitch for 16 rows

changing from black to white every 4 rows.

Cast off

Ears x2

Cast on 3sts in black

Row 1: Kfb, kfb, K1

Row 2: P

Row 3: k1, kfb, kfb, k2

Row 4: p

Row 5: k2, kfb, kfb, k3

Row 6: P

Row 7: k3, kfb, kfb, k4

Row 8: P

Cast off.

Tail

Using six strands of black and white thread, plait (in twos) for 5cm. Leave a further 5cm for end of tail. Tie a knot at the end of the plaiting and fray out the wool at the end of the tail using a needle. This gives a frizzy appearance.

Making up zebra

Sew up body from nose, under the neck and under the body, leaving a gap for stuffing. Fill with stuffing. Sew ears on to the side of his head. Sew up legs and fill with stuffing. Sew on to the underneath of the zebra. Sew on the tail.

Finishing off

Embroider mouth and nose using white wool. Cut circles out of white and black felt (using the template on page 91). Sew eyes on to the head using an overstitch and embroider a dot in the centre of each circle.

For the mane, use a big needle and 4 lengths of black wool. Start from the top of horse's head (between the ears). Make a stitch and leave a length of wool 2cm long each side of the centre of the mane. Cut the wool. Repeat all the way down the neck of the horse. Fray out the wool using a needle to make the mane frizzy (this also holds the wool in place).

Sew a pocket on to the back side of the zebra (using the same pattern as shown in planet a). Using two strands of double knitting wool, embroider the letter z onto the zebra.

Zip the zebra is zooming around. He's moving so fast his feet don't touch the ground. z, z, z, zoom

The Planet Phonics telephone

The 'phone allows you get in touch with Planet Phonics to send down a character which fits inside the rocket. The rocket transports the characters down to Earth from Planet Phonics.

Knitting pattern to make the 'phone

Cast on 16sts in 2 strands of turquoise yarn
Stocking stitch for 29 rows
Row 30: k (should be a purl row)
Stocking stitch for 7 rows
Row 38: k (should be a purl row)
Change to orange plus a gold yarn
Stocking stitch for 28 rows
Change to double turquoise yarn
Row 67: k
Row 68: k (should be a purl row)
Stocking stitch for 7 rows
Cast off

'Phone sides x2
Cast on 7sts in 2 strands of turquoise yarn
Stocking stitch for 29 rows
Cast off

Pocket for letter
Cast on 10 stitches in turquoise yarn
Stocking stitch 10 rows
Cast off leaving enough yarn to sew the pocket on to the phone

Making up
Make up the 'phone by sewing along the bottom seam and inserting the sides. Leave a gap to fill with stuffing. Insert a small bell. Sew up.

Sew the pocket on to the back side of the 'phone. Using two strands of double knitting wool, embroider the sound ph onto the knitted 'phone. Cut out the felt star, screen and white phone numbers using the pattern template on page 92.
Sew on to the 'phone using an overstitch.

Size
6 needles
Colours – double knitting yarn in turquoise and orange plus gold thread (knit two strands together to make a dense knitted fabric)

I'm calling Planet Phonics
on the Planet Phonics 'phone.
I've been calling up all morning,
is there anybody home?

I'm calling Planet Phonics.
Is there anybody there?
"Hello, you're sending baby bear?*
Oh great. Goodbye. Take care."

*or whichever other character is selected!

The Planet Phonics rocket

The 'phone allows you get in touch with Planet Phonics to send down a character which fits inside the rocket. The rocket transports the characters down to Earth from Planet Phonics.

Size 4 needles
Colours – double knitting yarn in blue (main colour), red and yellow

Knitting pattern to make the rocket

Starting at the top of the rocket
Cast on 6sts in blue
Row 1: [kfb] in all stitches (12sts)
Row 2: p
Row 3: k
Row 4: p
Row 5: [kfb, k1, kfb] 4 times (20sts)
Row 6: p
Row 7: k
Row 8: p
Row 9: [kfb, k3, kfb] 4 times (28sts)
Row 10: p
Row 11: k
Row 12: p
Row 13: [kfb, k5, kfb] 4 times (36sts)
Row 14: p
Row 15: k
Row 16: p
Row 17: [kfb, k7, kfb] 4 times (44sts)
Row 18: p
Row 19: k
Row 20: p
Row 21: [kfb, k9, kfb] 4 times (52sts)
Row 22: p
Row 23: k
Row 24: p
Row 25: [kfb, k11, kfb] 4 times (60sts)
Row 26: p
Row 27: k
Row 28: p
Row 29: [kfb, k13, kfb] 4 times (68sts)
Change to red
Row 30: k (should be a purl row)
Row 31: k
Row 32: p
Row 33: k
Change to blue
Row 34: k (should be a purl row)

Stocking stitch for 10 rows
Change to yellow
Cast on 6 sts (74sts) – (this makes a flap for the rocket opening)
Row 45: k
Row 46: p
Stocking stitch for 8 rows
Change to blue
Row 55: k
Row 56: p
Stocking stitch for 8 rows
Change to red
Row 65: k
Row 66: p
Stocking stitch for 8 rows
Change to blue
Row 75: k
Row 76: p
Stocking stitch for 8 rows
Change to yellow
Row 85: k
Row 86: p
Stocking stitch for 8 rows
Row 95: Cast off 6sts - Change to blue and knit to end of row
Row 96: p
Stocking stitch for 8 rows
Row 105: k
Change to red
Row 106: k (should be a p row)
Row 107: k
Row 108: p
Row 109: [k2tog] repeat to end of row (34sts)
Row 110: p
Stocking stitch for 4 rows
Row 115: [k2tog] repeat to end of row (17sts)
Row 116: p
Stocking stitch for 2 rows... continued on page 68

Rocket, rocket,
flying so high.
Zooming and zipping
past stars in the sky.

Wait, can you see
it coming down
to the ground?
If you're quiet
and you listen, you
might hear a sound.

Listen, listen, what
do you hear?
Someone is hiding,
can you tell who is near?

Rocket, rocket, who
do you hide?
Open the door and
see who's inside.

Knitting pattern to make the rocket continued from page 66

Row 119: [k2tog] repeat to last st, k1 (9sts)
Thread yarn through stitches and pull tight

Triangular side sections x2
Cast on 7sts in blue
Row 1: k1, kfb, k2, kfb, k2
Row 2: p
Row 3: k
Row 4: p
Row 5: k2, kfb, k2, kfb, k3
Row 6: p
Row 7: k
Row 8: p
Row 9: k3, kfb, k2, kfb, k4
Row 10: p
Row 11: k
Row 12: p
Row 13: k4, kfb, k2, kfb, k5
Row 14: p
Row 15: k
Row 16: p
Row 17: k5, kfb, k2, kfb, k6
Row 18: p
Row 19: k
Row 20: p
Row 21: k6, kfb, k2, kfb, k7
Row 22: p
Row 23: k
Row 24: p
Row 25: k7, kfb, k2, kfb, k8
Row 26: p
Row 27: k
Row 28: p
Row 29: k8, kfb, k2, kfb, k9
Row 30: p
Row 31: k
Row 32: p
Row 33: k9, kfb, k2, kfb, k10
Row 34: p
Row 35: k
Row 36: p
Row 37: 10, kfb, k2, kfb, k11 (27sts)
Row 38: p
Row 39: k
Row 40: k (should be a purl row)
Row 41: k19, skpo, k3, k2tog, k10
Row 42: p10, p2tog, p1, sppo, p10
Cast off

Side jets x2
Cast on 6 sts in red

Row 1: [kfb] in all stitches (12sts)
Row 2: p
Row 3: k
Row 4: p
Row 5: [kfb, k1, kfb] 4 times (20sts)
Row 6: p
Row 7: k
Change to yellow
Row 8: k (should be a p row)
Row 9: k
Change to red
Row 10: p
Row 11: k
Change to yellow
Row 12: p
Row 13: k
Continue in this way for 9 more stripes,
changing colours every 2 rows with the new
colour starting on a purl row,

Base of jet - in yellow
Row 32: k (should be a p row)
Row 33: k
Row 34: p
Row 35: [k2tog] repeat to end of row
Row 36: p
Row 37: k
Thread yarn through stitches and pull tight.

Making up the rocket

Sew in any loose ends. Sew down the back seam from the top of the rocket to the bottom leaving a gap in the middle from the top of the top yellow stripe to the bottom of the second yellow stripe. There is an overlap made by casting on six stitches. This is the door to the rocket which the characters can enter by. Sew a strip of Velcro on both sides of the gap or use poppers.

Make up the side jets by sewing along the back seam. Leave a small gap in the middle to put in the stuffing. Stuff the jets. Sew up the gap. Push in the base of each jet and using yellow thread stitch from centre of yellow base to the top. This forms a flat base.
Fold the triangular side sections in half. Sew up the base of the section. This forms a 3D triangle. Stuff the triangles and position both side sections to each side of the rocket. Sew the jets on to the triangular side sections.

Cut out the windows in black and white felt using the template on page 93. Sew on to the rocket using an overstitch. Cut the flames out of orange felt using the templates; six for the base of the rocket and three for the bottom of each jet.

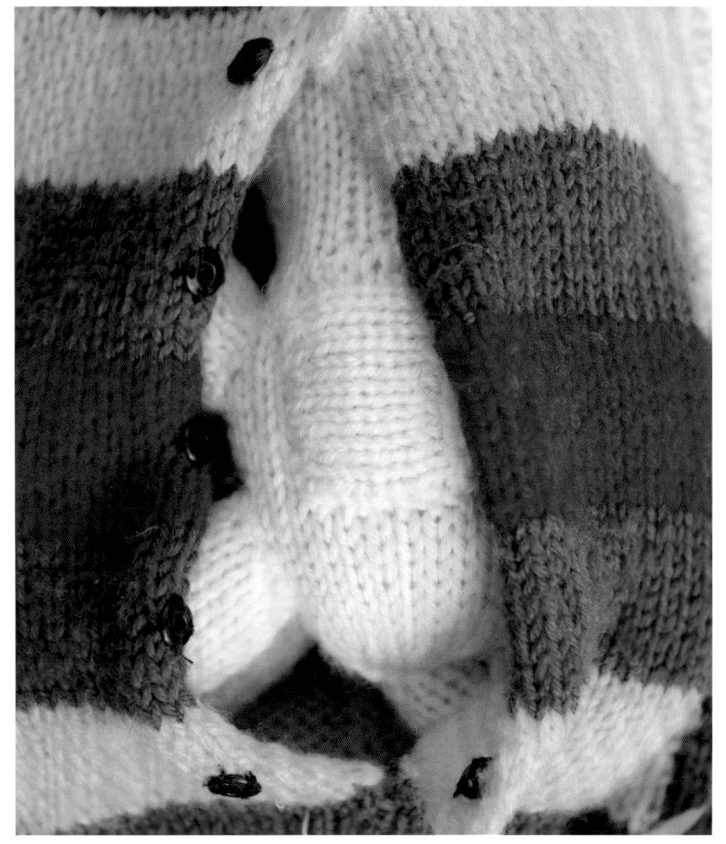

Useful information

Abbreviations

This list explains the abbreviations used in 'Planet Phonics Kniteracy':

approx	approximately
beg	beginning
cont	continue
dec	decrease
DK	double knitting
inc	increase
k	knit
k2tog	knit two stitches together (ie decrease by one stitch)
k3tog	knit three stitches together (decreasing by two stitches)
kfb	knit forward and back into the same stitch, and in so doing increase by one stitch
p	purl
p2tog	purl two stitches together (ie decrease by one stitch)
p3tog	purl three stitches together (decreasing by two stitches)
patt	pattern
rem	remaining
rep	repeat
skpo	slip one, knit one and pass slip stitch over
st(s)	stitch(es)

CRAFT CLUB

A national campaign for craft in schools

Craft Club

'Planet Phonics Kniteracy' is pleased to support Craft Club, the national campaign organised by the Crafts Council in partnership with the UK Hand Knitting Association and the National Federation of Women's Institutes, to encourage and promote the learning of yarn crafts, including knitting and crochet, to the wider population.

We'd like to see and help promote Craft Clubs in schools and libraries throughout the country, where volunteers teach people of all ages to learn to knit and crochet in a friendly, sociable environment (including the knitting of Planet Phonics characters and planets for local schoolchildren!).

Craft Club's ongoing 'Knit1, Pass It On' campaign is already proving how much children, given the chance, really enjoy knitting and crochet; how it provides a sense of achievement; boosts their coordination and dexterity; and how it can even help develop core skills such as maths and handwriting.

To find out how to get involved as a volunteer, how to set up your own Craft Club, or just to access some great yarn-craft resources, visit the Craft Club website at www.craftclub.org.uk

Yarn suppliers

While 'Planet Phonics Kniteracy' characters and planets can all be knitted from odd, left-over balls of wool or acrylic yarn, or even yarn which has been recycled (or unravelled) from old cardies or pullovers, you might want to buy some new yarn. With this in mind, here are the names and contact details of some of our favourite suppliers:

Cygnet Yarns Ltd
12-14 Adelaide Street
Bradford
West Yorkshire
BD5 6EF
tel 01274 743374
www.cygnetyarns.com

Patons
Coats Crafts UK
PO Box 22
Lingfield House
Lingfield Point
McMullen Road
Darlington
DL1 1YJ
tel 01325 394237 email
www.coatscrafts.co.uk

Rowan
Green Lane Mill
Holmfirth
HD9 2DX
tel 01484 681881 email
www.knitrowan.com

Sidar
Sidar Spinning Ltd
Flanshaw Lane
Alvethorpe
Wakefield
WF2 9ND
tel 01924 371501
www.sidar.co.uk

Knitting know-how

Casting on

The first step in knitting is casting on your stitches. There are several ways of casting on and we find the knitting-on technique to be both simple and versatile.

Make a slip-knot and place it on the left-hand needle.

Insert your right-hand needle into the loop of the knot and wrap the long-end of the yarn (ie that joined to the ball) clockwise around the tip of the needle.

Slide the tip of the right-hand needle downwards to catch this newly formed loop of yarn.

Place this new loop on the left-hand needle. Repeat this action until you have cast on the required number of stitches.

Basic stitch patterns

The stitch featured throughout this book is called stocking stitch and is made by knitting alternate rows of purl and knit stitches, with the knitted side forming the 'right side' of the finished character or garment.

Other stitches include reverse stocking stitch, essentially the reverse side of stocking stitch, in which the purl side is the 'right side', and garter stitch, which is created by knitting every row.

The knit stitch

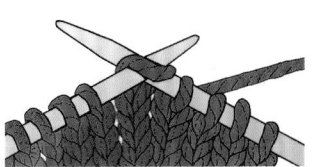 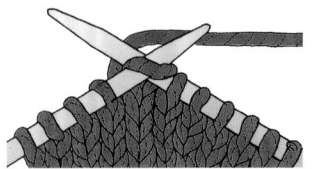 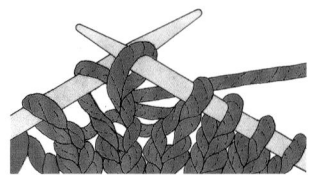

Having cast on, hold your stitches on your left-hand needle and insert the tip of the right-hand needle into the underside of the first stitch.

Wrap the yarn clockwise around the tip of the right-hand needle and in front of the tip of the left-hand needle.

Slide the right-hand needle downwards and catch the new loop of yarn you have just created ie a new knitted stitch! Repeat until the end of the row.

Knitting know-how

Basic stitch patterns

The purl stitch

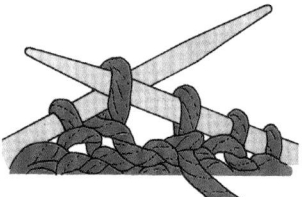  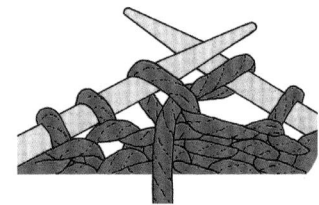

With your knitted stitches on your left-hand needle insert your right-hand needle into the front of the first of these stitches.

Wrap the yarn anti-clockwise around the tip of the right-hand needle.

Use the tip of the right-hand needle to pick up this new loop of yarn. This is your first purl stitch. Repeat until you have reached the end of the row.

Shaping

Decreasing stitches

Slip stitch decrease (skpo)
Knit along a row until you reach the stitch at which the pattern instructs you to start decreasing. Slip the next un-knitted stitch directly on to your right-hand needle and then knit the next stitch.

Using your left-hand needle, lift the slipped stitch over the knitted stitch and off the needle, to decreases your knitted work by one stitch.

Working two stitches together (k2tog)
Alternatively, you can decrease by knitting, or purling, two or more stitches together.

Increasing stitches

Working into the front and back of a stitch (kfb)
To create an extra stitch, and thereby enlarge what you are knitting, knit into the front of the stitch on the left-hand needle, and instead of removing it, knit into it again, through the back loop. Then slip the original stitch off the left-hand needle.

Casting off

This is what you do when you've finished knitting and want to secure your stitches and prevent them from unravelling.

Knit cast off

Knit two stitches and then insert the left-hand needle into the first of these stitches and lift it over the second stitch and off the right-hand needle. There's now just one stitch on the right-hand needle. Repeat the first step until all of the stitches have been cast off and then pull the yarn through this last stitch.

Purl cast off

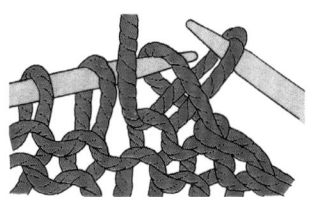

Purl two stitches and then insert the left-hand needle into the back of the first of these stitches and lift it over the second stitch and off the right-hand needle. There's now just one stitch on the right-hand needle. Repeat the first step until all of the stitches have been cast off and then pull the yarn through this last stitch.

Making up/sewing together

Mattress stitch is the perfect way of sewing together two pieces of stocking stitched knitting edge to edge – at the selvedges. When done neatly it provides an invisible, flat seam.

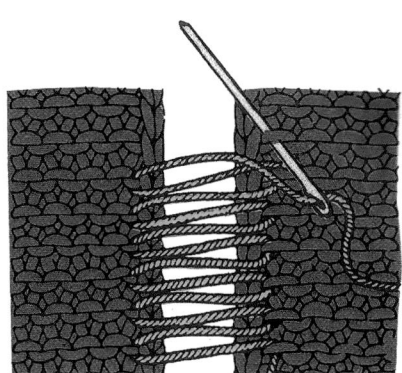

Use a blunt darning needle to avoid splitting your yarn and thread this with a length of the same yarn used for knitting the item you're sewing up (although the picture shows a different colour for clarity). Lay the pieces side by side with the right (front) side uppermost. Start the seam at the bottom edge by first joining the cast-on rows: insert your needle between the first and second stitch in from the edge, underneath one of the horizontal bars of yarn running between the stitches on one side, and then join it to the corresponding stitch on the other side and stitch upwards, picking up either one or two bars at a time, and pulling the thread tight every few centimetres.

a - The sneezing planet

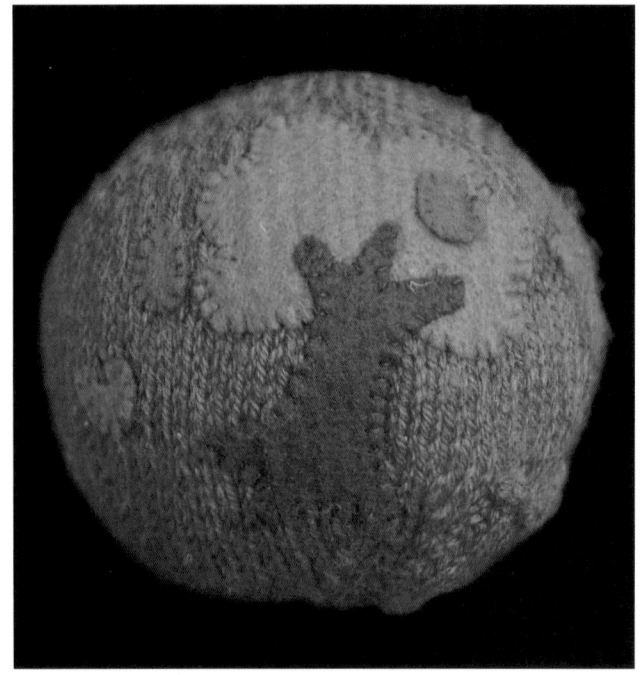

apples
3 green felt
3 red felt

tree top
green felt

overstitched in
fine brown thread

tree trunk
brown felt

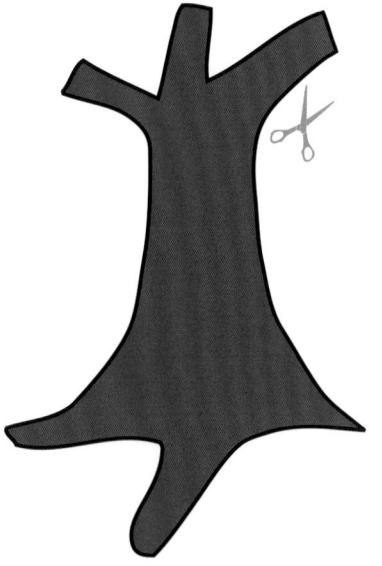

b - Bouncing bear

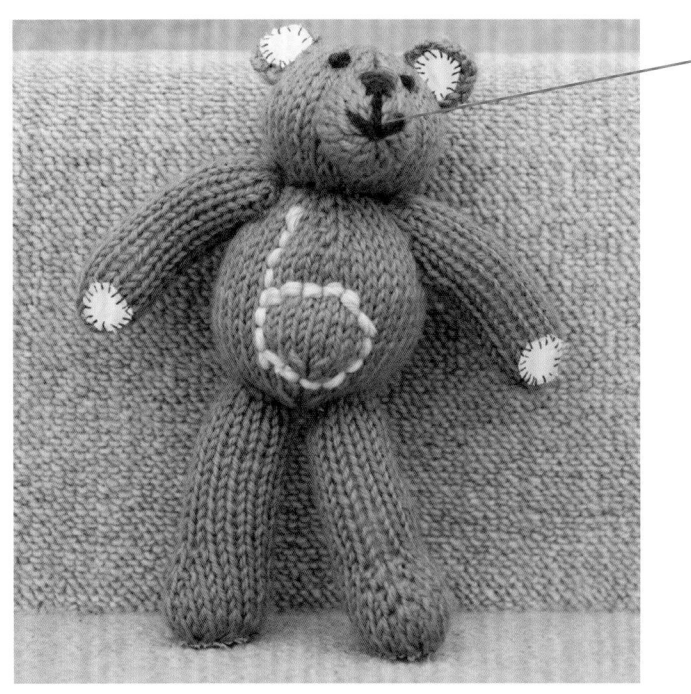

eyes, nose & mouth
brown wool

felt pads
optional

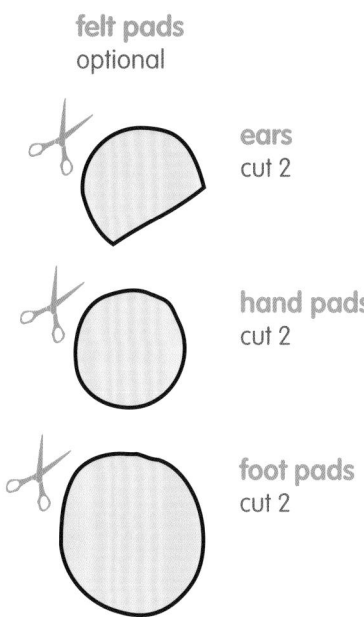

ears
cut 2

hand pads
cut 2

foot pads
cut 2

c - Clicking cat

eyes, nose & mouth
black wool

sew a white dot in
centre of eye in wool

camera details

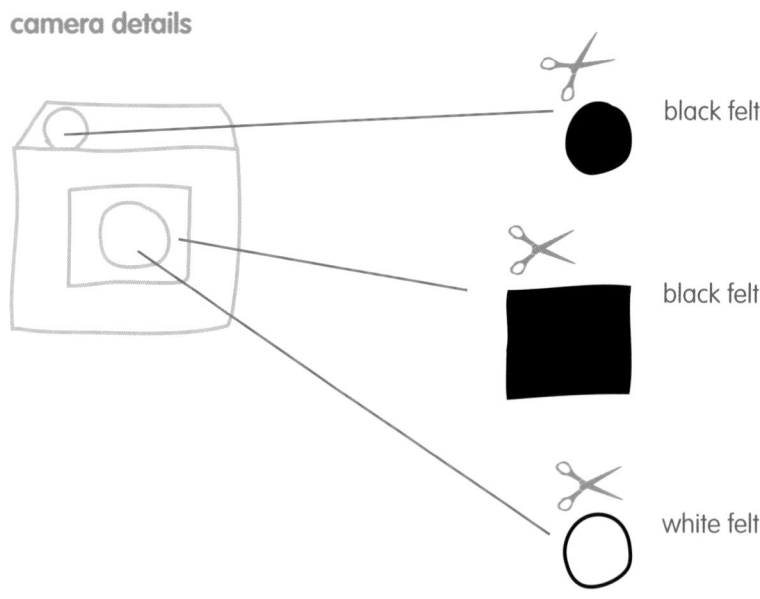

black felt

black felt

white felt

d - Dancing dinosaur

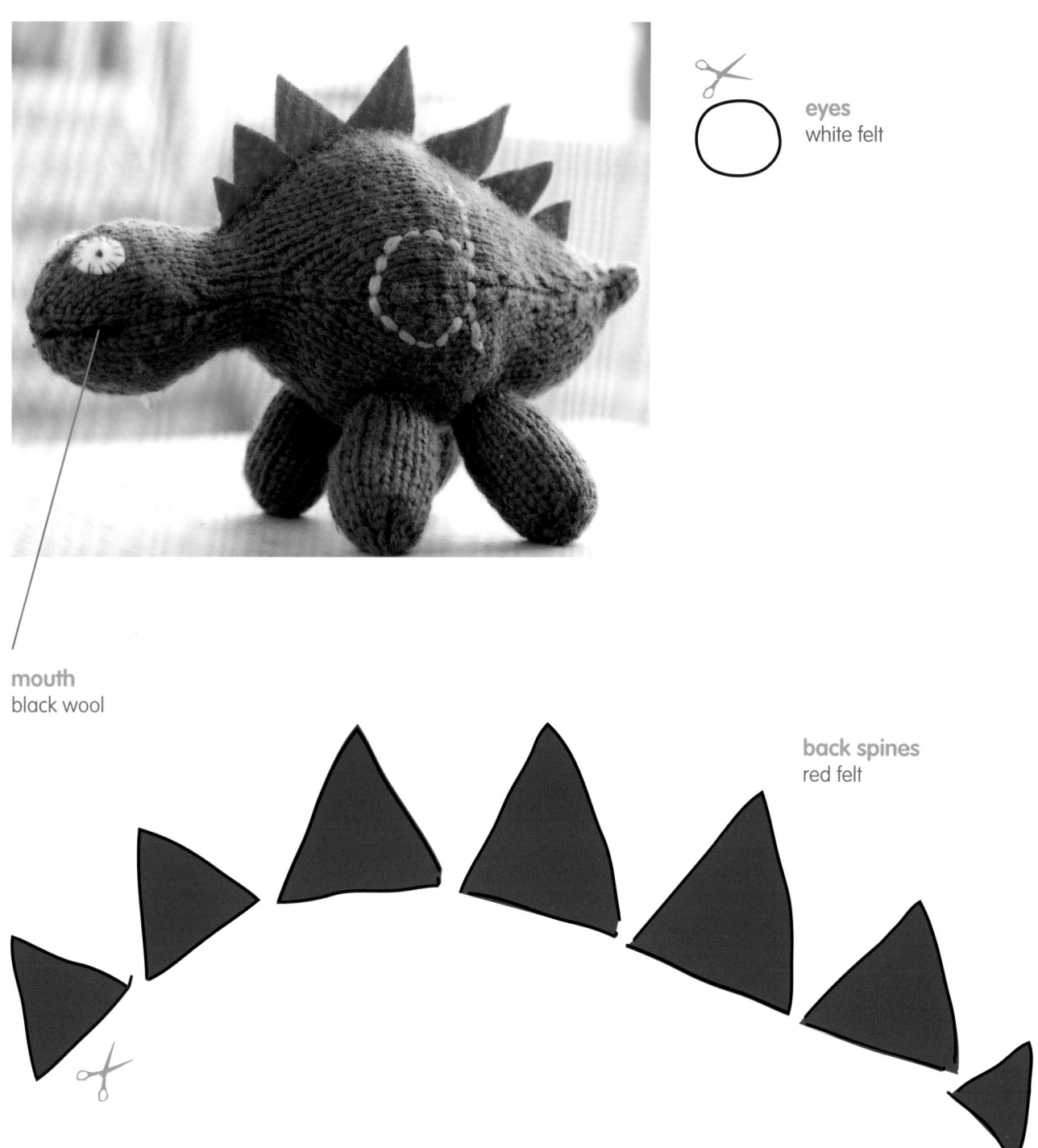

eyes
white felt

mouth
black wool

back spines
red felt

e - The exciting planet

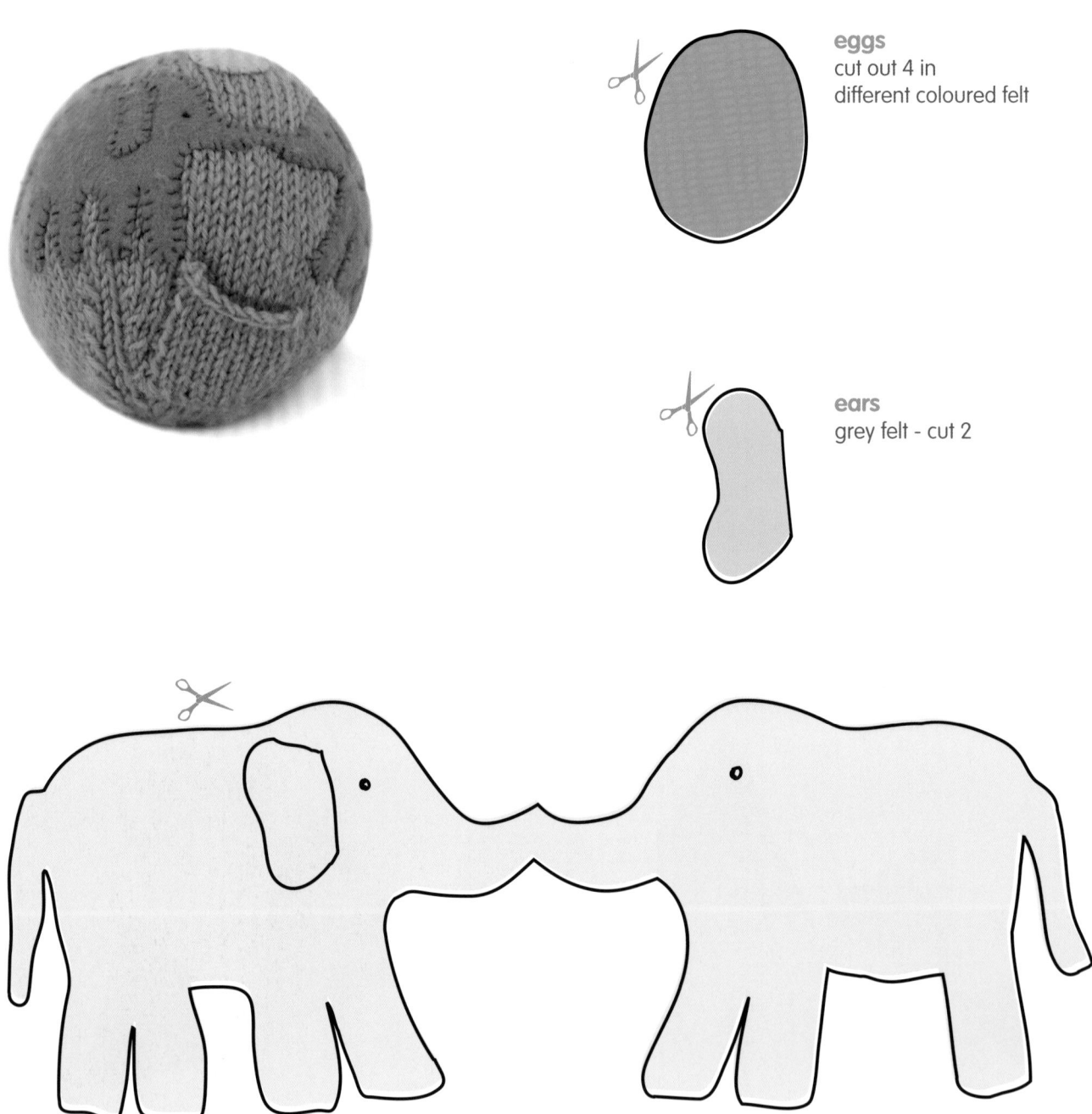

eggs
cut out 4 in
different coloured felt

ears
grey felt - cut 2

f- Freezing frog

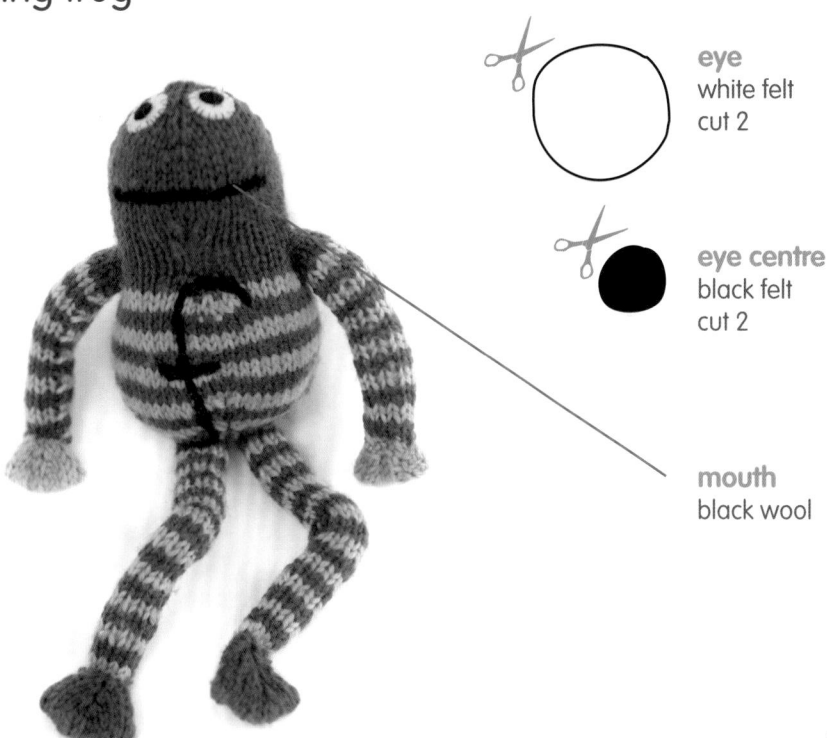

eye
white felt
cut 2

eye centre
black felt
cut 2

mouth
black wool

g - Growling gorilla

eyes
white felt - cut 2

nose and mouth
grey wool

Templates

h - Huffing horse

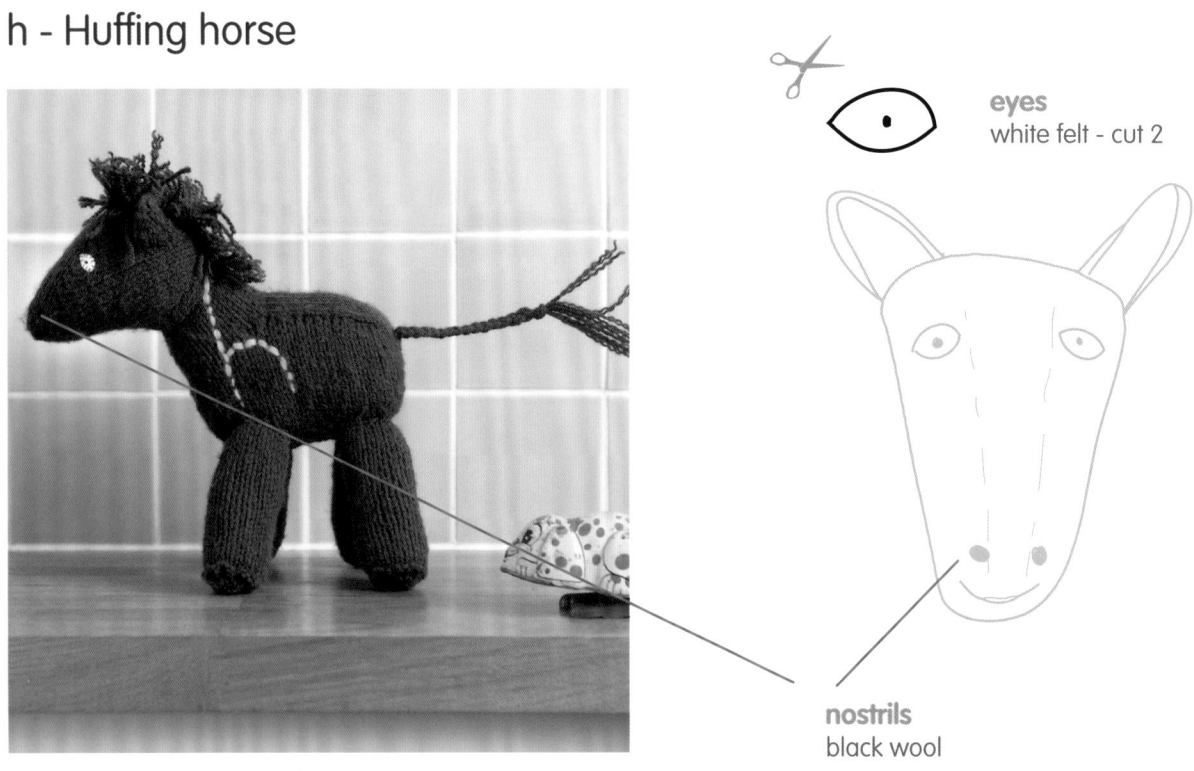

eyes
white felt - cut 2

nostrils
black wool

i - The itching planet

insects x7
black felt

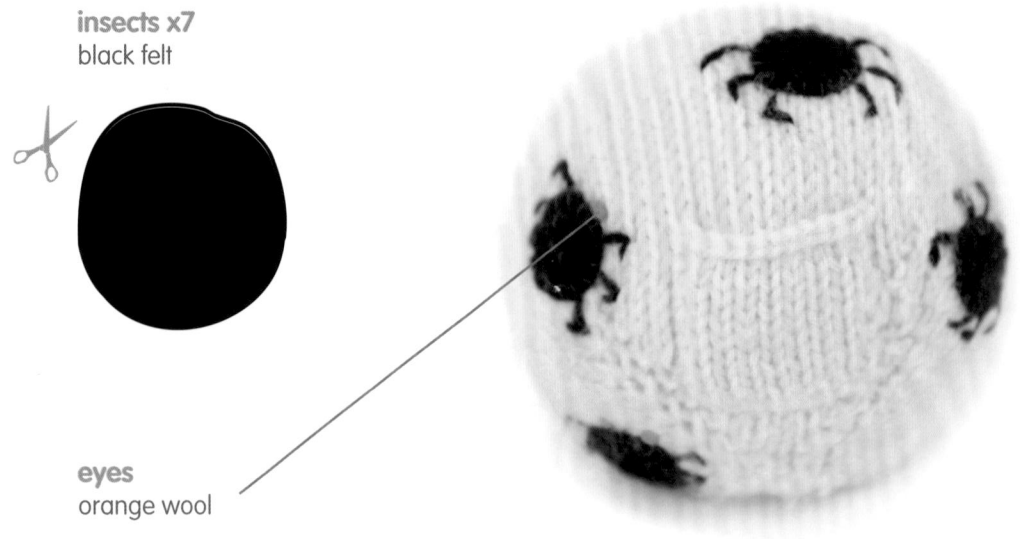

eyes
orange wool

j - Jumping Jack

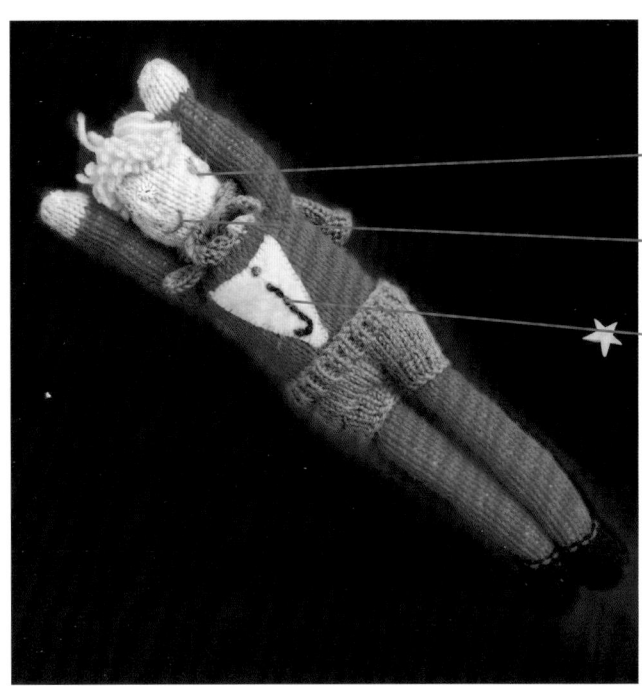

eyes
white felt - cut 2

pinched nose and ears

mouth
red wool

black wool J on yellow felt and back of cloak

Yellow felt - cut 2

k - Kicking kitten

eyes
white wool
eyes with
black wool
dot in centre

mouth
pink wool
mouth
and nose

Templates

l - Licking lion

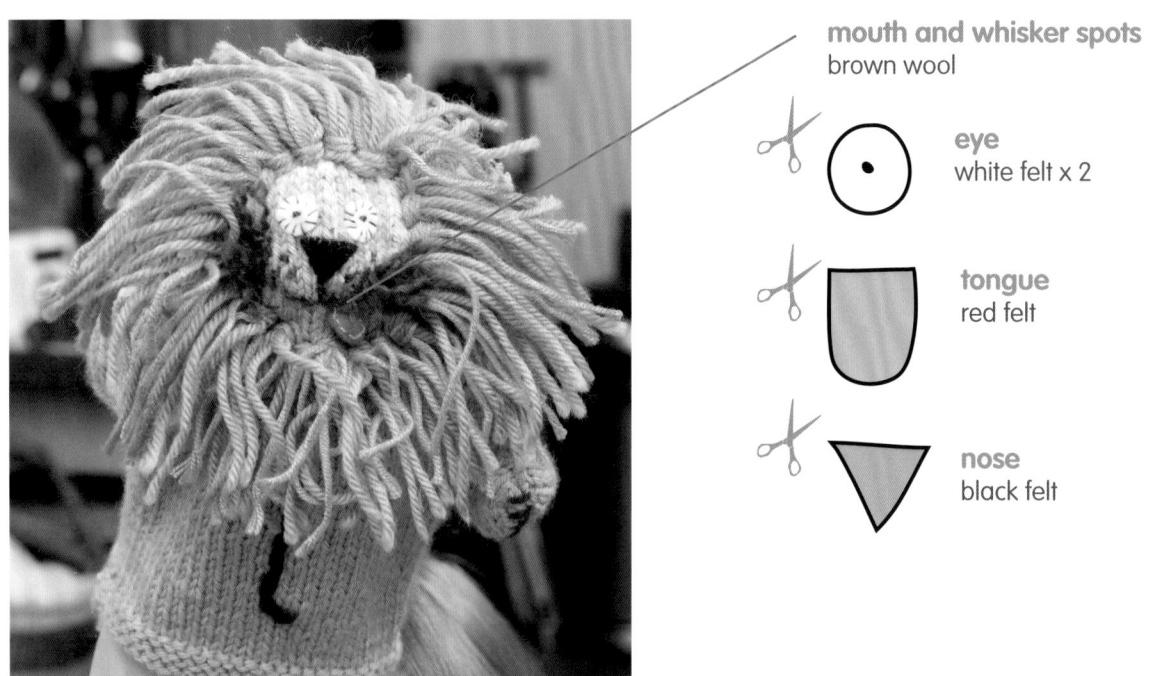

mouth and whisker spots
brown wool

eye
white felt x 2

tongue
red felt

nose
black felt

m - Munching monkey

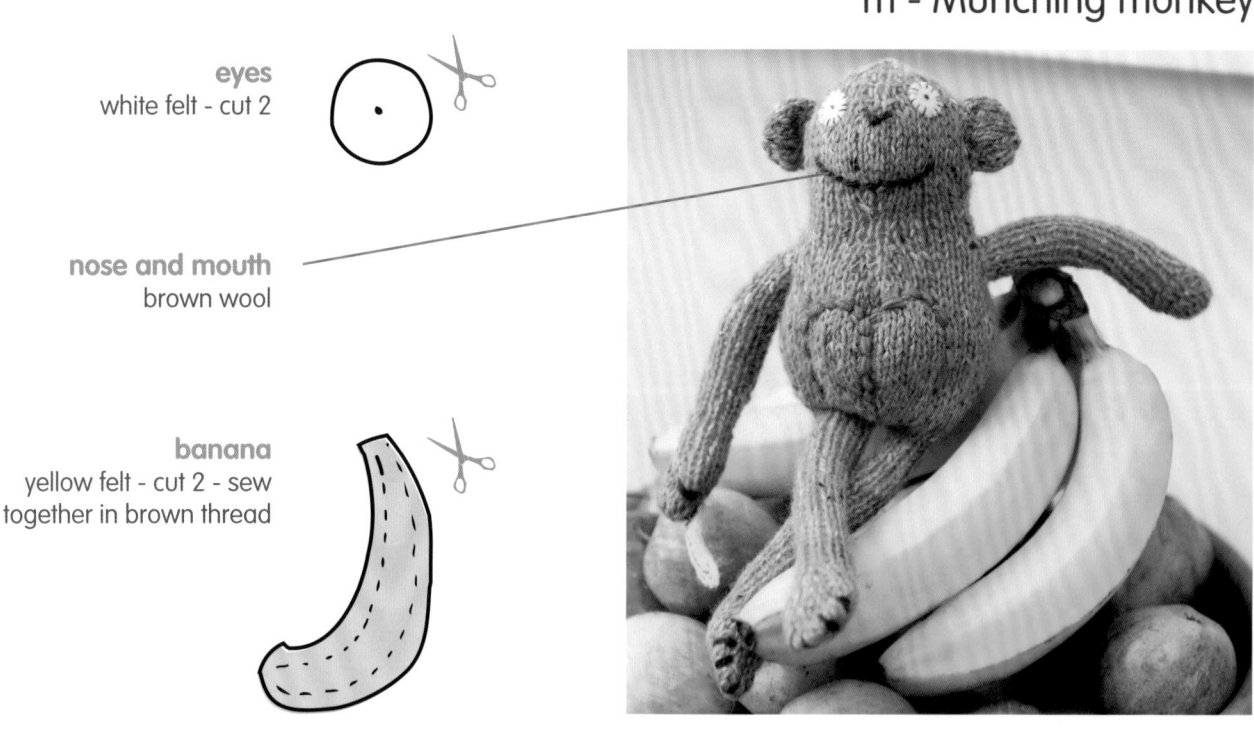

eyes
white felt - cut 2

nose and mouth
brown wool

banana
yellow felt - cut 2 - sew
together in brown thread

n - Nodding nurse

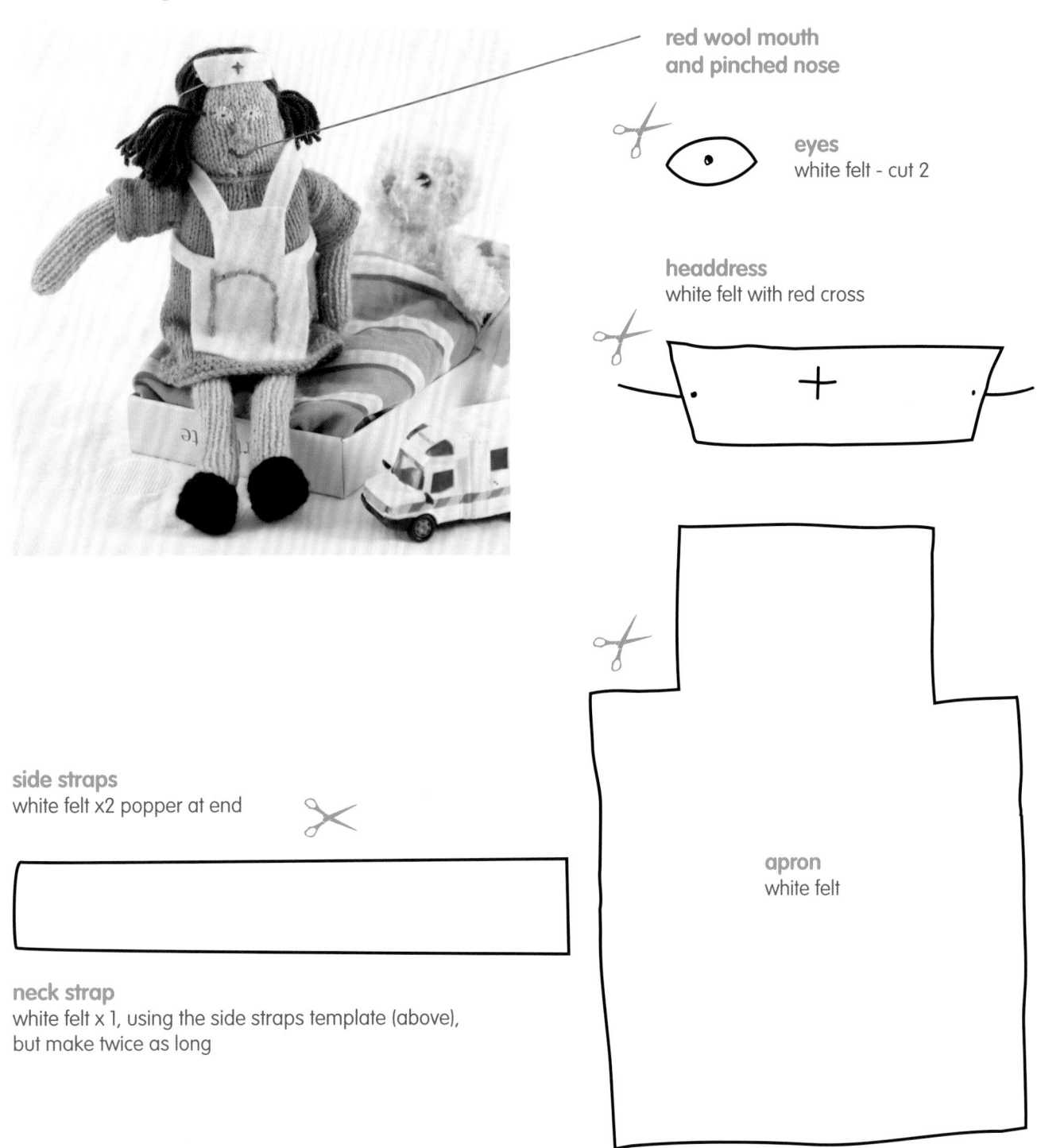

**red wool mouth
and pinched nose**

eyes
white felt - cut 2

headdress
white felt with red cross

apron
white felt

side straps
white felt x2 popper at end

neck strap
white felt x 1, using the side straps template (above),
but make twice as long

o - The octopus planet

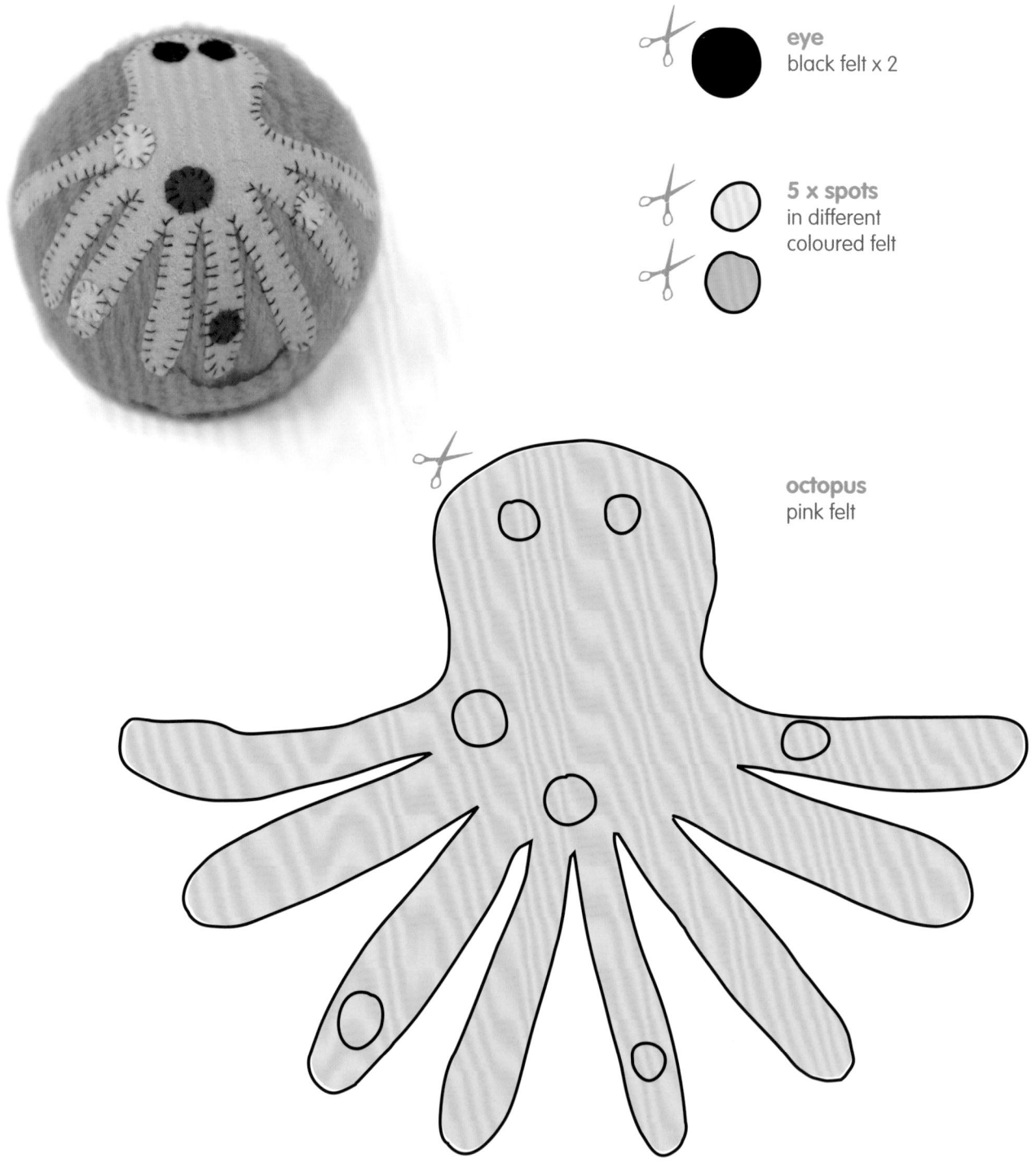

eye
black felt x 2

5 x spots
in different
coloured felt

octopus
pink felt

p - Popping pig

mouth and nostrils
brown wool

q - Quiet queen

crown
yellow felt -
stitched at back,
Velcro to fix on to
head

eyes
white felt - cut 2

**red wool mouth
and pinched nose**

r - Running robot

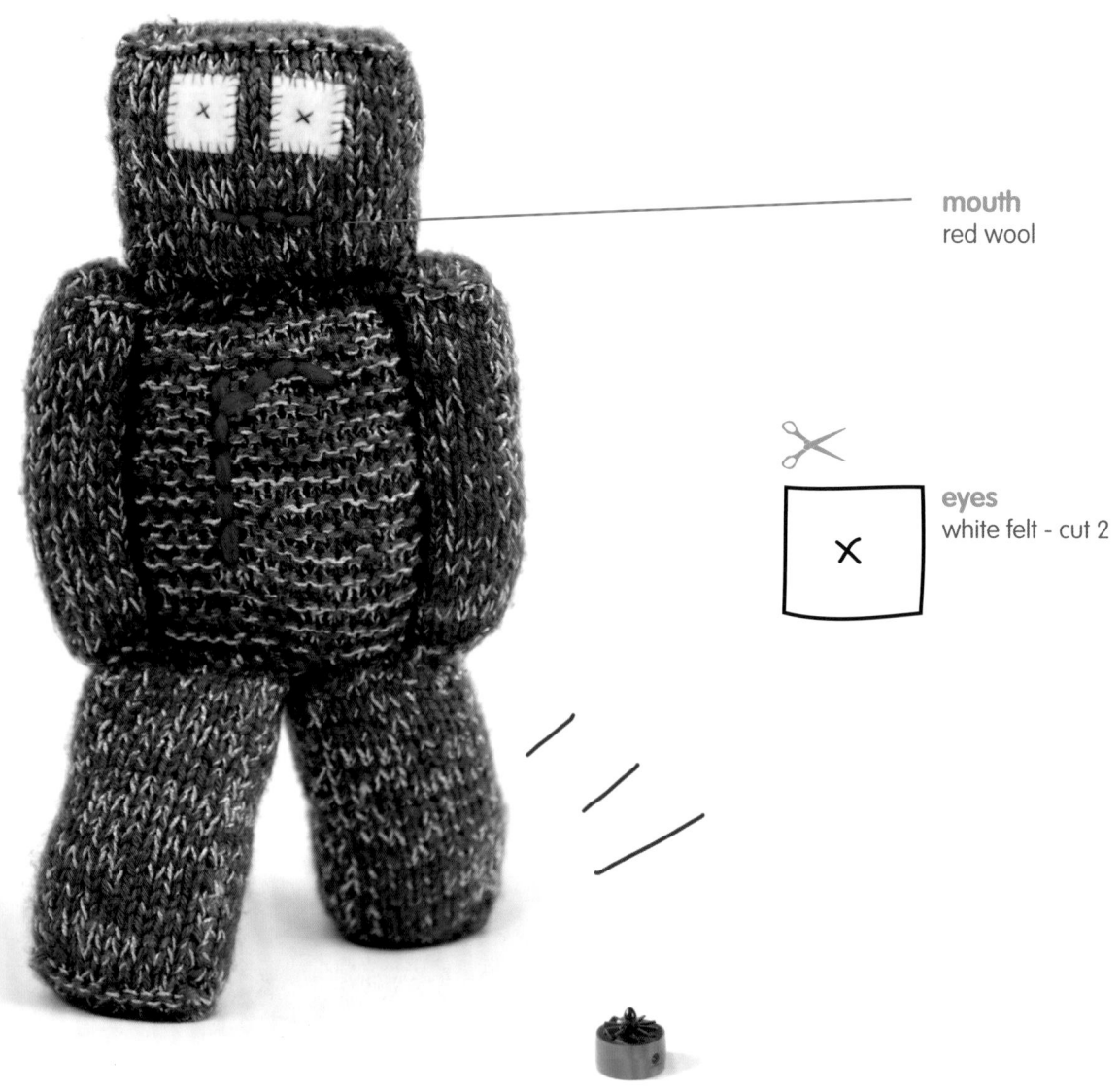

mouth
red wool

eyes
white felt - cut 2

s - Silly snake

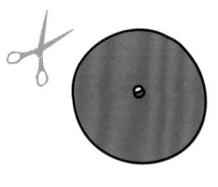

eyes
red felt - cut 2

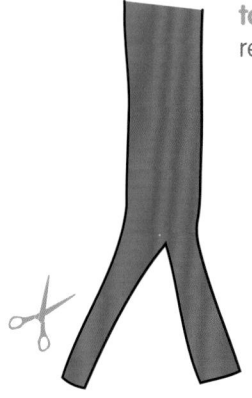

tongue
red felt

t - Ticking tiger

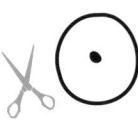

eyes
white felt -
cut 2

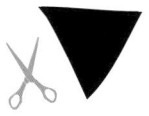

nose
black felt

u - The upside down planet

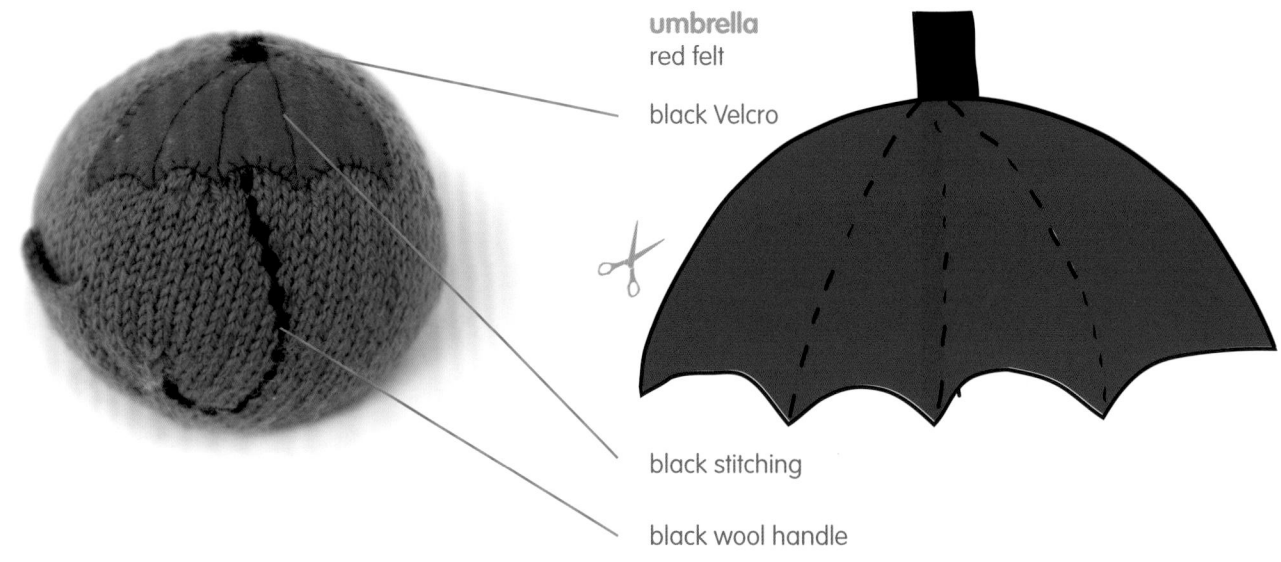

umbrella
red felt

black Velcro

black stitching

black wool handle

v - Val the vet

headdress
white felt with green 'vet'

thin elastic to go
around head

w - Wild witch

eyes
white felt- cut 2

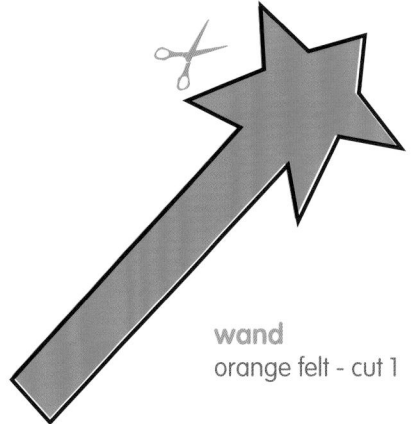

wand
orange felt - cut 1

base of hat
black felt

point of hat - sewn to base
black felt

Templates

x - Alien x

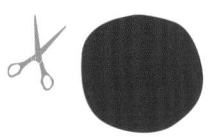

eyes
red felt - cut 2

eye centres
white felt - cut 2

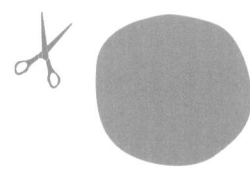

spots
different coloured
felt spots - cut 5

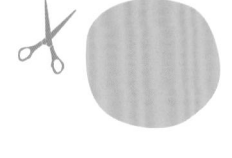

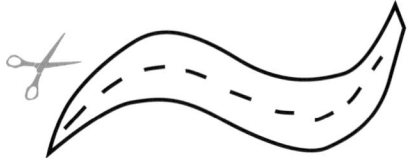

mouth
white felt
cut 1

hand
green felt
cut 2

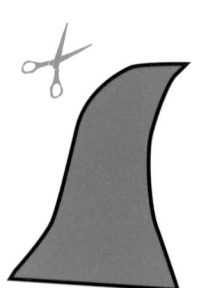

hair
green felt
cut 6

y - Yawning Yasmin

eyes
white felt - cut 2

mouth and nose
red wool mouth and
pinched nose, plaited hair

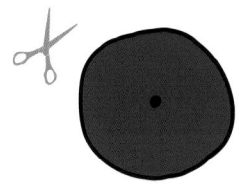

yo-yo
red felt - cut 2 and
sew together

6cm string to yo-yo

z - Zooming zebra

eye
black felt - cut 2

eye centres
white felt - cut 2

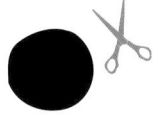

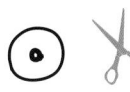

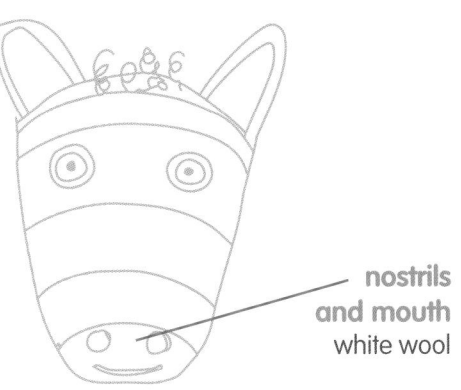

**nostrils
and mouth**
white wool

Templates

Planet Phonics 'phone

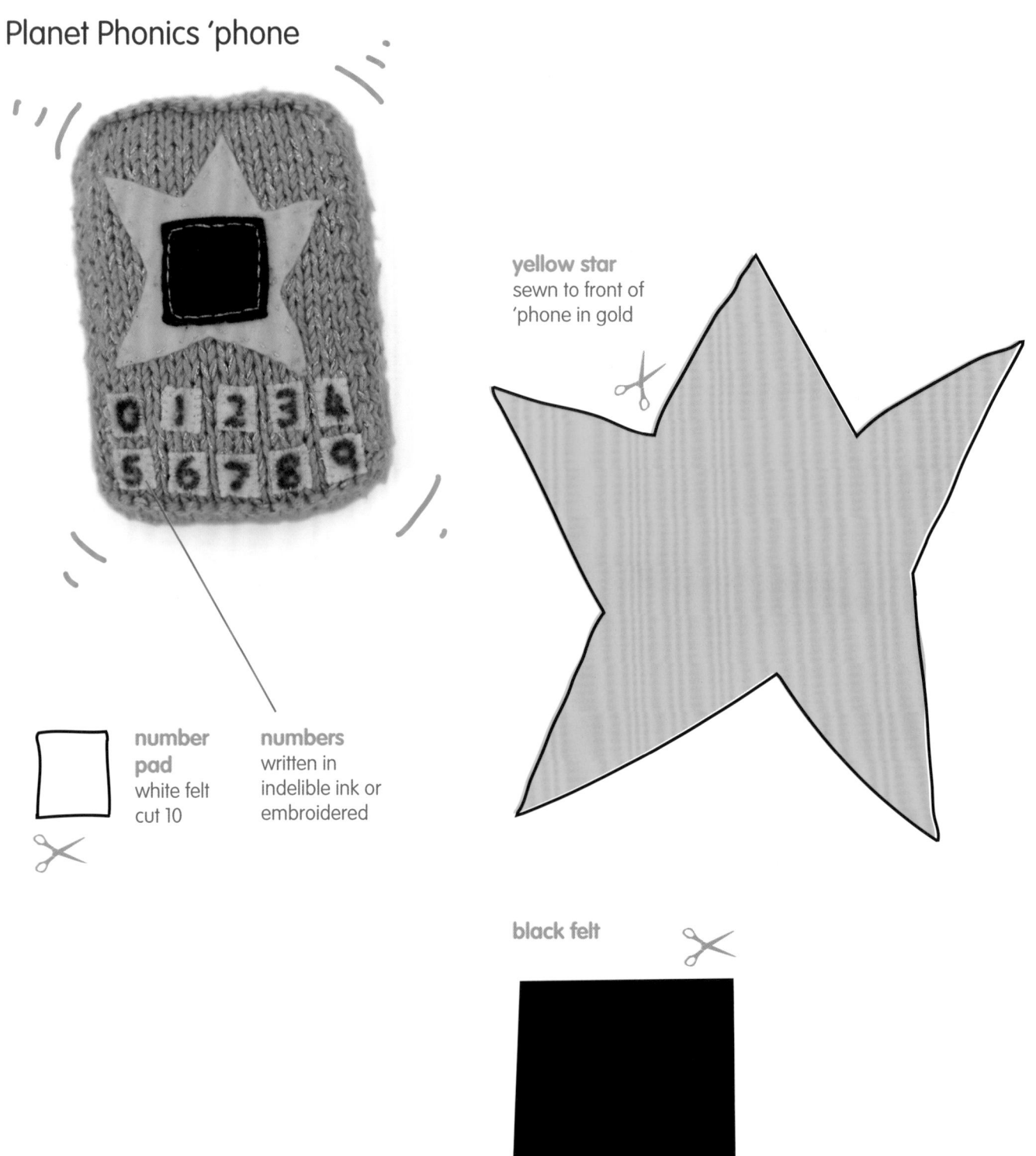

yellow star
sewn to front of
'phone in gold

number pad
white felt
cut 10

numbers
written in
indelible ink or
embroidered

black felt

Planet Phonics rocket

rocket windows
black felt - cut 3

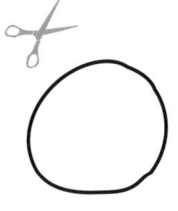

rocket windows
white felt - cut 3

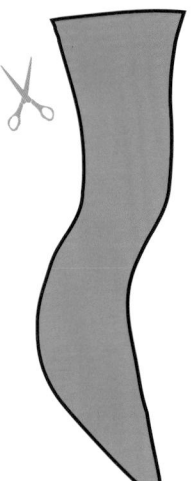

flames
orange - cut 12

6 for the bottom
of the rocket

3 for the bottom
of each jet

Letter templates

a b c d

e f g h

i j k l

m n o p

q r s t

u v

w x

Pocket letters

These letters are for you to photocopy and cut out. They are designed to fit neatly into the little pockets on the back of your Planet Phonics characters and planets. You could transfer them on to thick paper or card or even laminate them, for extra durability.

y z

Games

I Spy – easy game

You can play this with young children. Place a limited number of characters in front of the child - maybe just four or five to start with. Rather that saying the sound that the object starts with, describe it. This will help with the recognition of the characters. You can then show the child the letter on the back of the character.

Here are some examples:
I spy with my little eye someone who bounces down the stairs.
I spy with my little eye someone who is holding a camera.
I spy with my little eye someone who likes to dance.
I spy with my little eye someone who is brown and is huffing.
I spy with my little eye someone who is red and blue and is a super hero.
I spy with my little eye someone who likes to kick a football.
I spy with my little eye someone who licks his paws.
I spy with my little eye someone who munches bananas.
I spy with my little eye someone who always nods her head.
I spy with my little eye someone who wears a crown and likes the quiet.
I spy with my little eye someone who vrooms in a van and looks after animals.
I spy with my little eye someone who has a green face and waves a wand.

You can the play a normal game of I spy putting out a few characters. Take out the little sound cards from the pockets on the back of each character and match the character to the sound card putting the cards in the pocket as they are guessed.

Who am I thinking of?

For this game put out a few characters and take it in turns to ask the question:-

"What am I thinking of? It is a planet and it has apples on it."

The person who guesses correctly picks up the relevant character and appoints someone to ask the next question.

'Phone game (with rocket)

Use the 'phone to call Planet Phonics and the child can decide who is going to come down in the rocket. Use the rhyme on page 65.

Character/Sound Matching

Choose a few characters. Take the cards out of the pockets. Spread the characters and the cards out over a table. Take it in turns to pick up a character and find its sound card. Put the card back in the pocket as it is matched to its character. Take it in turns to pick and match.

Alternatively you can spread out the sound cards, pick one up and say: "What character starts with this sound?" When the character is said, the child can have it and put the card back in its pocket.

Rocket game

Hide the characters inside the rocket and say the rhyme on page 66. The child has to guess who is inside the rocket.

Making words

Lay out the characters and ask the child to make simple three-letter words such as cat, hen, pit, dog and mud, using the characters or the sound cards.

Kim's Game

Put six or seven characters on a tray or just on the table and let everyone study them for a few minutes. Everyone then closes their eyes or turns away and the person in charge takes away a character. They then have to deduce which character is missing.

To make the game harder put out more characters or remove more than one.

Planet Phonics Kniteracy and beyond...

'Planet Phonics Kniteracy' is the first of a series of books designed to help children learn the sounds necessary to read and write.

A second knitting book will help children to learn more complicated sounds, such as the long vowels, sh, ch, th, wh, ng, ar, or, ou. This second knitting book features knitted characters arranged in themes. The first of these is The Farm with adorable characters such as Cheep the chick and Shep the sheepdog. The Circus features King Kong, the strong man and Ow the clown. The Pirates include Captain Jake, Pete the pirate, Slime, Jones the bones and the Cube. These themes work with the long vowel planets and their stories.

Two other very important books tell the stories of all the characters as well as introducing songs and games. The first of these features the characters we first meet in 'Planet Phonics Kniteracy' and will be illustrated throughout by Pip Adams. There are detailed stories for each of the characters. Songs are included to reinforce the sound each character makes and its action. A CD of these songs will be included in the book. There are also games, raps and lots of ideas to bring the characters to life.

The second illustrated story book provides stories, songs and background on the characters featured in the second knitting book.

And in addition to all this, we will also be producing a series of small illustrated phonetic reading books featuring all the Planet Phonics characters.

Debbie Long, August 2012

a b c d e f g h i j k l m n o p q r s t u v w x y z